Picking up the Pieces

"Healing from life's betrayals"

Transitioning from being a victim to survivor

Written by Stephan Skotko

ISBN-13:978-1469949017
ISBN-10:1469949016

All photos used are personal or by way of public domain

"Take pictures boys and take plenty of them, because one day some S.O.B. is going to say this never happened and try to deny history"

-1945, General Dwight D. Eisenhower addressing his troops upon the liberation of Auschwitz Death Camp in Poland at the end of WWII.

Table of Contents

__Introduction__

By Mr. Gale Millard, Bend Oregon

September of 2008, was when Steve was thrown into his insane, horrible, journey. At the time, he telephoned me from Oregon, where he was living with his family. I was living in Florida retiring to be near some old friends and family, enjoying life in the sun.

Steve was in near panic when he called me. He told me of the horrible things he had been accused of; he was absolutely distraught with anguish. I felt helpless as I listened to him pour out his heart. He spoke for a very long time as he shared with me the insane things Knox had convinced his family of.

Naturally, I was incredulous at the scope of all the horrible things Knox caused, using Steve's entire family against him. Steve's subsequent arrest and his being booked into jail on the false accusations, further led to his attempted destruction. Steve's total being was torn apart by the obviously uncaring and dangerous Marion Knox.

I have known Steve for over eleven years. During this time I have come to love and respect him. I feel his connection to our Lord is very secure, strong, and directly included in his daily walk. In 2008 I began encouraging Steve to begin a journal about his life. I told him he might want to write a book someday about what had happened to him; about the dangers of seeing a phony family counselor. Steve did indeed write a book when he moved to Ohio to reconnect with his Mother and family in 2009.

I was able to help Steve after he was finished writing his first book, *A Heart Held Ransomed.* I had the distinct pleasure and opportunity to spend many hours with Steve, proof reading the book several times, to be certain, it was exactly what he wanted to say and how he wanted it said. This was done over the telephone and took several weeks.

I am now doing the same thing with this second book, *Picking up the Pieces*. The difference here is Steve asked me to write the introduction for him. I wish I could tell you how honored I am to be asked to do this. I am very proud to call Steve Skotko, my friend and brother in Christ.

As we fast forward to the present time, I would like to suggest to you, the reader, if you haven't read the first book Steve wrote, *A Heart Held Ransomed*, may I humbly suggest you get a copy and read it. This way, you can get a full descriptive narration of the full accounts of the accusatory atrocity, of how it all began. It will explain the beginning, all in plain English. Once you have read and understand it, then this book will make so much more sense to you.

Picking up the Pieces, is a well written, step-by-step instruction of how one gets past the pain and into the healing process. It is written using Steve's love of history. It will bring about your full understanding of the hows and why's Steve used in his own healing process. It is an interesting book simply based on history. However, it goes far beyond this particular realm, and uses the process of invention, which applies it to practical uses in our daily thinking patterns.

Jesus is the main person and healer of our minds, souls, and bodies. He is our rock and our salvation. He tells us plainly: "We can do ALL things, thru Christ, who strengthens us". This means we CAN heal. We CAN be free from all pain and strife, which would come upon our lives.

__Acknowledgements__

I want to dedicate this book to my children, Carolyn, Wesley, and Zachary, whom I have been estranged from for over three years. I love the three of you more than you will ever know. This book is dedicated to the three of you and to the day we again see each other; to the day when you will realize and see the reality of the unorthodox theory of repressed memories. I will always love you unconditionally. I will do all within my power until the day I die to bring individuals who teach this bogus repressed memories into accountability. No one will hurt them the way you three have been hurt.

Thank you to my friend Gale, my mother Dorothy, Uncle John and all my friends in Pueblo, Colorado at Victory Life Ministries for the support, texts, and encouragement they give me.

Thank you to my pastors Darin and Gloria Carroll of Victory Life Ministries. I extend a special thank you to Edward and Rothel LeCompte, Pastors of Bethel Baptist church of Plainview, Texas, for their support, friendship, and stepping forward to host my very first book signing! I appreciate you!

Forward

By Pastor Darin Carroll
Senior Pastor; Victory Life Ministries, Pueblo, Colorado

There are too many "Christian counselors" who have used this title to achieve wealth, fame and recognition, or as in this case, to destroy lives and families! I believe the church body needs to stand up against sin and the defilement of Christians within the body. We have tolerated seeker sensitivity and have been so politically correct we have forgotten we serve a Holy God! I am proud to see Steve stand up against the enemy and say, enough is enough; I refuse to stand back and let the enemy come into the body of Christ and "steal, kill, and destroy" any more families!

There are a few, who will question Steve's reasoning for taking on this challenge; to stop not only Mr. Knox, but, any other fraudulent "Christian counselors". I have known Steve Skotko for over 30 years. He has taken on this challenge for one reason, because he is a Christian, which believes you do what is right because it is right!

The damage has already been done in Steve's life and family. Only by a complete miracle from Jesus Christ will Steve's situation be brought back to what it was. Steve is bravely fighting for the countless victims who could possibly be affected in the future by these fraudulent "men of God." I believe in deliverance counselors and Christian counselors only when he or she can base their advice and their methods upon the infallible word of God...THE HOLY BIBLE!!! For anyone out there that has been a victim of fraudulent "Christian counseling," this book is a must read!!!

With Jesus, ALL things are possible! Steve shares the

difficulties and the pains, which he went thru and goes thru. More importantly, he shares how his relationship with Jesus brought him from a place of utter destruction; from a place where the enemy thought Steve was down for the count, into not being just a survivor, but to a place of being more than a conqueror in Christ Jesus, a Victor! Steve has been brought to a place of healing, blessing, and victory in Jesus!

Just like Thomas Edison, Steve has not looked at his difficulties or losses as failures or wasted time. Steve has viewed them as stepping stones and opportunities for God to use his life in yet another way; a catalyst, if you will, from being a victim to a Victor! When Steve chose to step out of the darkness and expose the strategies of hell designed to destroy families, he took the power and control away from Satan.

Since then, countless people have been encouraged to step out and speak up against the lies' of the enemy, which was trying to neuter men and women of God! Through the power of Jesus Christ, we are seeing people's lives restored, healed, and they are taking back their dignity! Once again they can walk in victory with Jesus. With their heads held high they proclaim boldly to the world and to the enemy.

"There is No weapon forged against me which will prosper, and EVERY word, which would rise up against me in judgment, shall fail!!!"

Thank you Steve for laying out your heart, your hurts, and your experience for all to see; because of this many will come to know the wonderful healing power of Jesus Christ!!!

I love you my friend
Pastor Darin Carroll

<u>Chapter One</u>
The Beginning of the Transition

"All greatness of character is dependent on individuality. The man who has no other existence than, which he partakes in common with all around him, will never have any other than an existence of mediocrity."
– James F. Cooper

"I haven't failed; I just found 10,000 ways, which don't work." Thomas Alva Edison is best known for his discovery of the incandescent light bulb. Edison was an American inventor, scientist, and businessman who developed many devices, which greatly influence life around the world today. These inventions include the phonograph, motion picture camera, and a long-lasting practical electric light bulb.

Edison was dubbed "The Wizard of Menlo Park" (now Edison, New Jersey) by a newspaper reporter. He was one of the first inventors to apply the principles of mass production and large teamwork to the process of invention. Therefore, Edison often receives credit with the creation of the first industrial research laboratory [1].

Edison is considered one of the most prolific inventors in history, holding 1,093 US patents in his name, as well as many patents in the United Kingdom, France, and Germany. He is credited with numerous inventions, which contributed to mass communication and in particular, telecommunications

Previous to Edison's discovery of the light bulb, most of the world's lighting came by way of gas lights. Everything concerning light and lighting we enjoy today was once provided by gas. Homes, businesses, and even traffic lights were powered by gas. The consumer had to light every device by hand. The fashion in which homes today are wired, were in Edison's time fitted with gas pipes.

Traffic lights were located on poles, which were placed on the street corners. These were then lit and extinguished by human hands for as long as the need arose. A Caution light meant these street lamps were not lit because the worker had finished his duty day; hence the term "caution." Today we motorists enjoy those caution lights as flashing and hanging from the wire in the intersection.

With Edison's discovery of the light bulb also came a device in which the individual could turn it on and extinguish it. Edison's production factory created over 50,000 incandescent light bulb lamps the first year alone. These discoveries came with a huge amount of retaliation by the gas companies who monopolized the market on home lighting.

Edison's discovery of the light bulb and the application of electricity dramatically changed the face of the modern world during his time. With Edison's discovery came a relentless barrage of opposition to his modern day utility empire. Edison came against huge odds, assaults on his character, family, and experiments.

Yet, Edison still prevailed. He refused to quit, and he refused to surrender to the abuse he received. Today the world enjoys all of his inventions. For the most part we all take for granted what was once considered a miracle. It makes you stop and think, how many things I take for granted today, were a miracle to someone in the past!

Edison refused to quit

In studying Edison, what inspires me the most is what I have just stated, he refused to quit. He refused to be trapped in his failures, opposition, and the preconceived views and ideas of other men. He had a vision. Setbacks, preconceived views, and failures did not diminish Edison's vision. He knew how to defeat his personal demons of discouragement.

Edison believed in his vision. In fact, he looked at his failures not as failures, but in ways not to do things. Edison was accused of many things but he was a pioneer in his life time. Many today reflect back and accuse Edison of being, "Cut-throat, ruthless, and unscrupulous" in his business practices. Yet they cannot deny, nor can they do without Edison's discoveries.

Once my ordeal began it took a while to encourage myself to not be a victim of my circumstances, but to step forth and succeed. I will admit there was a time when I felt totally discouraged and defeated. At times I lay in bed and would pray to die!

I still do deal with my personal "demons" of discouragement; I just knew what needed to be done. I came to the realization if I did not muster the courage and step forward, and tell my story, many more people would be hurt and devastated by the same sort of "therapy" my family received.

God gave me a vision, and placed a calling upon my life. It is like a football game. You don't always score a touchdown. Sometimes you have to punt and play defense. I make myself remember there are two teams going at it to win. Both teams play against the clock. In doing these things and taking these steps in my life, I refused to become a "professional victim." I refused to remain a victim of abuse. I refuse to be defeated. I will triumph!

Am I comparing myself to Thomas Edison? Yes in a way I am, as I try to learn what I have studied about him. What I am saying is we all come against times in our lives where we have to dip way down into ourselves and pull out a winner's attitude. I am fascinated by stories in history like this. I have learned a tremendous amount and gained insurmountable wisdom along the way.

In the autumn of 2009 I was speaking with a friend who had gone through a similar experience as me. I was half way through my story to him when he stopped me and said, and I will never forget it,

"Steve, Steve, stop! You don't have to say any more and I am going to tell you this only once. This trial is too big for you to carry it on your shoulders. Give it to God and let it go. You are just one member on the team. God's shoulders are best prepared to carry this."

"So let God do it!"

Those words so impacted my life. I decided right there in the midst of my hurt, disappointment, and feelings of betrayal, to let my situation cause me to be better and not bitter. T.D. Jakes states,

"If people want to exit or leave your life, then let them go"

It is not easy to do and it does not happen overnight. It's a slugfest with your personal demons bent on destroying you, bent on demoralizing you! Almost always your personal demons wear the mask of those you love, trust, and never would you think would betray you!

Those are tough words to accept when you have been hurt; when you have been cut to your core. I think we can all apply this statement to whatever situation would rise up against us!

Decide to be better and not bitter!

There comes a time in every one of our lives when we are faced with a serious question or line of questions; these can be times of hurt, times of betrayal, and times of sacrifice. Notice the word "bitter" has the letter "I" in it!

It is in these times when we have to dig way down and decide how we are going to conduct ourselves. We need to think clearly and realize at any time and with every decision, we will ultimately have to live with our decision for the rest of our lives.

In the end we control our own destiny and the path we set ourselves on and what we can accomplish. The decisions and actions of others may force us into these times of heart wrenching despair. But in the end it is our choices no matter the circumstances, we will live with!

Sometimes you have to do things you've never done to reach a place you've never been. These new places are where you will find your healing. If you stay in the old place, then you will become a "professional" victim. Sometimes life will throw you a curveball, and then sometimes the pitch is to close, and you get drilled in the head!

Professional Victims

Why are some people such great victims? Why have they chosen to become "professional" victims? Why do they choose to stay in the same place and never move forward? It's like they relish the pain and suffering. They cherish their abuse. There are very likely some old files (people) in their life, which tell them:

"You need to suffer to be good."

"Good people suffer and wicked people prosper."

"Nobody loves you, hugs you or kisses you when they think you are not abused, sick, or ignored."

Do you see how these beliefs will fuel the fire of victimhood? Ask yourself this question, do I enjoy being a victim? What is it about the drama, the pain, and the struggling of being the victim, which you believe makes you need to hang on to it?'

If you think you need to be crucified to be seen as good, godly, accepted, or righteous, then you will sabotage yourself every time. Why wouldn't you?

If you're subconscious mind links suffering and pain to being "good enough, saved, righteous, and spiritual," then you will do a mighty fine job to achieve **your** goals! Look carefully at what your motive is behind your playing victim and decide whether or not you are ready to let go [2]. This is the crux of it; you have to decide to let it go. You decided when it started, and you will decide when it ends!

They hurt me; I didn't do anything to deserve this treatment

Being a victim is not what it's cracked up to be. Picking up the pieces of your shattered life; nothing in this world can describe it. There is not one professional individual alive, which can fully understand the pain of being a victim of abuse, unless they have been abused themselves. Based on this, **you** are the only one who can decide **when** it will stop.

No matter what the level of their education is, they will never fully understand your pain; how can they? This is why you have to go somewhere you don't want to, in order to receive what you need.

You are a unique individual. Scripture tells us the following in Psalms 139:14 (NLT),

"I praise you because I am fearfully and wonderfully created. Your works are wonderful, I know full well."

We are all unique individuals. You are a matchless individual. You are wonderfully made. The Psalmist declares "I am fearfully and wonderfully made." There is not another individual alive or has ever lived or who will ever live, which will be exactly like you. Only you can accomplish what you are destined for. No one else will accomplish your goals. My ordeal has been placed before me, and God has given me all the equipment I need to achieve the outcome He desires.

My decisions on this journey will determine the outcome!

My decisions!

Whatever may be your belief system, all would have to agree the human body is quite unique. The human spirit is inimitable, and the human mind is unconquerable. If you have studied any sort of science about man, everyone would agree the conception of the human being is quite remarkable, it is peerless. Even today geneticists are baffled at the random chances of the embryo. You are wonderfully made. I believe God has a design on each and every one of us.

Psalm 139 goes on to say even more things about us as individuals:

¹⁵ *You watched me as I was being formed in utter seclusion,*
as I was woven together in the dark of the womb.
¹⁶ *You saw me before I was born.*
Every day of my life was recorded in your book.
Every moment was laid out
before a single day had passed.

¹⁷ *How precious are your thoughts about me, O God?*
They cannot be numbered!
¹⁸ *I can't even count them;*
they outnumber the grains of sand!
And when I wake up,
you are still with me!

There is not another person who has lived your life; therefore nobody can make decisions for you. We are all unique individuals. We all have unique sets of circumstances we have all endured. We have all made choices, which produced each and every one of the outcomes we have experienced in life.

I truly believe where we enter into error is letting someone else make decisions for us. This is why being psychologically abused is devastating because you begin to give in to the abuser. You begin to live the lie they are forcing onto you. They violate your will and self esteem. In essence you surrender your uniqueness and let yourself be put into a mold. Literally you are like a robot. You cease to think, you cease to react, you cease to reason, and you cease to be unique.

You lose respect for yourself. When you enter this arena it fuels the abusers fire; when they know or sense you don't respect yourself. Once you are no longer in your psychologically abusive relationship, you still have to retrain your mind and break the mold you have been in. This can take time. This is the hardest thing you may ever have to do.

When you accept your circumstances then you can build your future. When you confirm you are right and begin to have self respect, then you co-operate with others automatically, it comes easy. Then you, being yourself, will begin to help others be themselves. Your abuser will no longer be able to dominate or control you.

I never want to cringe before anyone ever again. I want to respect other individuals, and I want them to respect me. People who abuse don't respect you. They respect nothing.

Abusers are obstinately defiant towards authority. They do not value you as an individual. They do not respect your individuality. Individuals, who abuse, seek to control and dominate.

Taking all this into consideration, we have the makings for a wonderful life. We can attain anything, which is set before us, no matter the circumstance, person, or event. The strength to overcome is available. Life is wonderful and it is a gift from God.

"Your life is a gift from God. What you do with it is your gift back to Him."-Billy Mills

Mean People

There are mean people in the world, bent on enforcing their will on others, they are abusers. Familiarize yourself with this fact. There has always been and there always be mean abusive people. As long as there are mean abusive people in the world there will be wars. There have always been wars and there will always be wars, unless people are willing to respect and accept other people as unique individuals.

Researching my personality

I still think of the period of my life when I had the opportunity to travel through Eastern Europe. My ancestral roots are from the Slavic regions of Eastern Europe and Western Russia.

I toured former concentration camps, Nazi officer camps and historic castles, churches, and fortresses. I have always been a World History and World War II buff. I grew up looking at maps of the region.

Maps fascinated me. My interest was always peeked to this part of the world. I always had an inner draw to this region of the globe. I would sit and look at maps for hours on end. I still do today when I get the chance.

I have always loved looking at maps and watching over time as boundaries changed. From the conquering hordes of barbarians to the Nazi blitzkrieg, I was fascinated how they so quickly could ravage the land.

It was such an uplifting portion of my life seeing and witnessing all the landmarks of Poland, Germany, Russia, Ukraine and the Czech Republic.

Some of my favorite times were wandering the streets of small towns and villages and mingling with the people. Walking with them and mixing with them gave me a familiarity with people, which were similar to me.

Shopping in the markets and mixing with the locals was exhilarating for me. Had not my grandparents made the decisions to immigrate the way they did, I could very well still be living and functioning as those I was observing. Had they not immigrated to the United States I very well might not even exist.

This is the power of making decisions. Touring these lands helped me understand who I really was, my personality, and thought processes. I always knew growing up, one day I would visit and visually witness firsthand these lands and the monuments they had to offer.

I did not see all I wanted, but I saw enough to help me realize who I was. I discovered I am a unique individual. The same power in making decisions lies in each and every one of us. Our decision no matter how minute, greatly determine the actions others will take and the decisions they will make.

It was not until September of 2008 I became aware I was a victim of abuse, and had been for quite a number of years. At first I did not realize this or even make note of it. Over time I began to realize the impact of the decisions of others, which were part of my life.

I did not do anything to warrant the barrage of assault, which was beginning on my life. Those who would perpetrate the abuse upon me might very well tell you something different from their perspective.

With ample time to contemplate my situation, meditate, and pray, I drew similarities to what I had educated myself with over the years, in my studies through history. Similar to the start of World War

II, there were signs, growing pains you may say, indications of what was about to transpire in my life. For years prior to the Nazi war machine rolling into Poland on September 1, 1939, there were all kinds of signs, eminent doom, and worldwide pain was about to be felt by all.

For years previous to the official start of World War II. Hitler made advances in Europe and consumed countries without a fight. The world surrendered countries to Hitler to keep the peace. The world was not ready to engage in another world wide altercation.

In my life those who perpetrated the abuse required portions of my individual life, which I freely surrendered to keep peace in my home. This is what abuse does to you. You sacrifice portions of your life to keep the peace until you either cannot or will not sacrifice any further. At this point the battle ensues. The war begins.

This sort of thing happens a lot in church atmospheres. Leadership requires a tremendous amount from those too young to amply carry the load, all in the name of God. Today the effects of World War II are still present in our lives. Millions of people are dead because the world failed to recognize the "devil for who he was."

Think about it, millions of people died at the hands of Adolf Hitler and others. People, who had futures as doctors, lawyers, and other professions, were never able to make the contributions to society, which they were called to do.

Their lives ended in a gas chamber or they were burned in an oven. I visited Auschwitz. I saw the ovens. I stuck my head in one. The human protein deposits are still in those ovens, like plaster of the walls of homes to this day.

I saw the stacks of eyeglass frames, the piles of human hair, and the bins full of the soles of shoes. They are there to this day as a memorial to those who perished because the rest of humanity would do nothing to stop the madmen!

My uncle whom I am very close to these days was a soldier in World War II. Although he does not actively speak of his experiences, he has commented from time to time of them.

These comments have left me with the impression it impacted his life greatly. How could it not? Even my mother remembers he was different once he came back from the war. Just those brief views into his conscious mind and his comments affect my life.

During this time in our history people for the most part paid little or no attention to Adolf Hitler and the German Nazi army. They all knew it was there and governments just fed the growing beast to pacify it and keep it at bay. Hitler abused the world long before the war began. The world did nothing to stop him until it was totally threatened by him.

Most countries were beginning to recover from the great depression and their focus was inward. The world was still reeling and healing from the effects of World War I.

There was revelry and social partying everywhere in the world. The roaring 20's brought a relief from the victimization of the world from World War I. The world during this era had been raped and left to burn. They even referred to World War I as the "Great War to end all wars." Germany under the Kaiser had raped and pillaged Europe.

The Kaiser in fact abused Europe and beat it to a pulp. The world at the time of 1919, and 1920 was transitioning from being victims to being survivors and finally being the victor; in surviving came a time of gratification and social accomplishment.

The industrial revolution of the early 20th century had yielded things, which took war to new heights; literally with the aces in air warfare of World War I. Germany lay in ruins, ashes, and great economic distress as the rest of the world partied during this time. This distress gave rise to a worse beast, which was Adolf Hitler.

As the world transitioned into the 1930s the great depression struck the world; a complete opposite of the prior decade. Individuals stood in "bread lines" where literally a loaf of bread cost a day's wages.

Men went from being accomplished business entrepreneurs to jumping out of windows to escape the pain, which lay in front of them. It was not a pretty period of time, so I am told.

It was during these events people like my uncle lived. When the threat of war came they stood in line to enlist. We all admonish and respect these men and women who gave their lives for their country. Today our country has erected numerous monuments to their heroic endeavors. I truly believe I have and still can learn a lot about myself and life from studying these events and this period of history.

George Santayana said,

<u>"Those who do not learn from history are doomed to repeat it."</u>

This is why I compare these examples of history to my life. If I don't learn from history I will repeat these same things in my own personal life. Times are different, but the perpetrating devils are the same and they wear the same masks! This is why General Eisenhower told his men to take pictures and take plenty of them. He understood one day the outlook of mankind would change; mankind would try to deny what took place in Nazi Europe during World War II.

Likewise, we can claim the same for our lives. If we do not learn from our lives we will be prone to repeat the mistakes of our lives. If I pay no attention to those around me and the mistakes they make, I very well could make the same mistakes. If we choose to remain victims we will forever remain victims and never become survivors.

I emphatically believe the generation of my uncle witnessed the effects of World War I, lived through the roaring 1920s and the great depression of the 1930s and wanted nothing to do with another world dictator such as Adolf Hitler. At first I believe they just chose to ignore what was happening; hoping it would just go away. So why did the world feed this "beast" until it got so big it cost millions of people their lives in order to stop it?

The individuals of this time failed to learn from their history and then were faced with the realization it was happening all over again and wanted nothing to do with it and fought back. However, I believe the world waited too long to respond. In not reacting sooner millions of lives were lost as a result of the barbaric treatment of the Jews and other socially threatening individuals; at least those Adolf Hitler considered a threat.

At one point in the mid 1930s boatloads of Jews left Germany for the United States to flee the oppression and upon arrival were turned away and forced to return to, which inevitably sent them to their deaths in concentration camps.

What this says to me is the world did not want to deal with issues. The world including the United States did not want to accept the fact what they were witnessing in Germany was the rise of another Mad Man. This I believe is why Eisenhower did what he did. He witnessed this denial first hand and saw the results of that denial.

It is a delusion to think by denying or ignoring problems and issues they will go away and cease to exist, thus the example of World War II. It is a grave error to not change and to curl up in a ball and only exist in your own world. It does not solve anything. It only breeds and feeds the out of control beast in our lives; bent on destruction and further abuse.

My ordeal, which began in September of 2008, left me faced with two choices:

1.   Curl up in a ball, put my head in the sand, and lick my wounds.

2.   Or fight back and refuse to not be just another victim.

I could receive the boatloads of refugees (my hurt), deal with them and liberate them in my life or send them back to their prisons. I didn't want and I do not want to be a victim any longer. I want to be a survivor.

What catapulted me to being a "survivor?" I believe it was the fact I refused to fall into the status quo of victims. Instead I decided to fight back and make a difference. The only thing I had was my relationship with God. The only thing I had was my life. I wanted to make my life count. I felt God's encouragement to fight through the war, one battle at a time. I still want my life to count.

The thought of doing nothing to stop the perpetrators in my life haunted me. The thought of another family, another man, another father losing all he has just did not sit well in my heart. I knew the more I did the less likelihood of this happening again would be true.

I failed to recognize the abuse transpiring in my life for well over 15years before 2008. I waited too long, lost everything, and then began to react only because I had to. I had issues while still living in Colorado. I did not deal with those issues.

What I did instead was flee to Oregon in an attempt to start over. The problem was, I went with me, and nothing really changed. All I did was change the oil in the car of my life. I did not make the necessary repairs.

I attempted to rebuild my life on an old foundation. A foundation, which I did not realize was always going to be with me. When I left Colorado in 1998, I did not know I was a victim of abuse. I did not "recognize the devil for who he was."

When my circumstance came full circle and slapped me in the face in 2008, I began to realize I was a victim of abuse. I knew I did not want to be a victim, I knew I wanted to be a survivor. The Hitler in my life had achieved too much power and control. Only a war would exorcise it! Once, you have reached the survivor plateau, the sky is the limit. I want to graduate to the next level and this is being a victor. To walk in total victory no matter what my past may have dictated at one time.

Through the time since 2008 I have fought numerous battles in my war. Time will tell who is right and who is wrong concerning my life and the circumstances I am facing. The men in my life, which I respected and trusted over time turned out to be controlling and contemptuous. They left me to die on the battlefield.

Those men and those I am referring to as the perpetrators more recently, who let others control them into making the false accusations against me, know who they are. They are individuals who are not able to face their own shortcomings and sin. They are shallow individuals. They merely place blame on others. This can and usually does bring a brief period of relief. The problems resurface again for them because they have not dealt with their own self.

I really don't care what they think. Individuals, who believe the other side against me, have this right. I don't care what they think anymore, and in reality it is none of my business what they think. It is of no avail to me. It does not matter to me if they agree with me, or ever choose to reconcile. I pray every day we may reconcile. If they choose not to reconcile, this is all right in my books.

As I stated, what they think or believe are no longer any of my business or concern. In a way I am grateful for them. All this pain they chose to afflict on me has caused me to grow as a person. They have made their choices. I love them, and always will. I respect them as individuals and whether or not I agree with their decisions is of no avail.

I will always be opened hearted to them and receive them back. They chose to leave and I leave it up to them to choose to reenter my heart when they decide.

<u>"It is not about how hard you get hit, it's about how hard you get hit and continue to move forward."</u>

In the book of my life I am moving forward!

Notes Chapter One

[1] Walsh, Bryan. "The Electrifying Edison." Web: Time July 5, 2010

[2] http://www.janjanzenministries.com /newsletter
       DoYouLikeBeingTheVictim.pdf. Retrieved January 25, 2011

Chapter Two
You are in Total Control

Orville and Wilbur Wright are credited with inventing and building the world's first successful airplane. The Wright Brothers receive credit for making the first controlled powered and sustained heavier than-air human flight on December 17, 1903. [2]

In the following years the Wright brothers developed their flying machine into a fixed wing aircraft, which was the first of its kind. What most people do not realize is they were not the first to fly an aircraft; others were unable to sustain their aircraft for any period of time. The Wright brothers invented the first controls, which made it possible for fixed wing air flight. [3]

What is most interesting is the Wright brothers researched and developed the three-axis control, which enabled the pilot to steer the aircraft effectively. This permitted the pilot to maintain balance and equilibrium. This theory is still standard in today's aircraft engineering.

From the onset of the Wright brothers work and aeronautical research, they wanted to develop a reliable method by which the pilot is in total control of his circumstances and outcomes. This would solve the flying problems, which were beginning to be associated with flying during this era.

This approach differed significantly from other experimenters of their time. Other aircraft engineers were placing more of an emphasis on more powerful engines. The Wright brothers believed in strong engines but, the power and control of the entire aircraft should be placed on the pilot rather than external forces. [3]

The Wright Brothers gained the mechanical skills essential for their success by working for years in their shop with printing presses, bicycles, motors, and other machinery. Their work with bicycles in particular influenced their belief that an unstable vehicle like a flying machine could be controlled, balanced, and mastered with practice. [2]

From 1900 until their first powered flights in late 1903, they conducted extensive glider tests. These tests developed and honed their skills as pilots because gliders rely on a single individual in control. Their bicycle shop employee Charlie Taylor became an important part of the team, building their first aircraft engine in close collaboration with the brothers [3]. Together they incorporated engine power into their aircraft after they tempered their flying skills.

If I had listed this book as helping to "recover from abuse or an abusive situation or relationship," most people would not buy or read it because a lot of people have the wrong perception of abuse. Most people who suffer from abuse would say they have never been abused, or are in an abusive relationship or situation. The emphasis of this chapter is determining what abuse is. This was my situation. For years I would have looked you straight in the eyes and deny I was being abused. I shockingly came to find out I was!

This is the same with flying an aircraft. You can't just buy a book on how to use the controls of an aircraft in order to learn how to fly. You have to learn aerodynamics. You have to first learn how to recognize the forces, both seen and unseen, which would come into play when flying an aircraft. You have to be able to perceive any eventual outcome at any time, and respond to it lest you crash and burn.

So how do the Wright brothers fit into the definition of abuse? It is not so much about abuse but in order to get out of it, you will have to take charge of your circumstances. You have to be able to recognize the forces, both seen and unseen, which have led you into your current situation. You have to see things for what they are and are able to perceive an outcome.

Life is lived by trial and error

Most of the things we do in life, took trial and error to learn. It is inevitable; you will fail at some point in life and probably miserably before you succeed and accomplish your goals. I know I have at many times, as I did not perceive things correctly and most certainly did not have the correct outcome.

Just as a child when taking his or her first steps, you will fall flat on your face many times before you ever succeed at anything. I really have a desire and a burden to reach suffering individuals. Those who feel trapped in their circumstances, minds, and hearts from the abuse they have suffered. I truly know and I really understand, because I have been there. You are being abused if you feel like you are not in control of any situation you are experiencing!

I know what it is like to feel total despair wondering if I would ever make it and wondering if I was going crazy; wondering if my present mistake, would take me out permanently. There have been times my pain was so deep, I felt as if I were in a pit. The more I scratched and clawed my way out, the deeper it felt I was sinking and getting buried by my situation. When I would look up I would see the ones I loved the most throwing shovels of dirt on me.

Reaching out

I really want to reach out to men who have been falsely accused. I know there are a lot of them out there. Many of them are forced to live a difficult life because of their circumstances, because of the accusations. We suffer through the barrage of accusations. People who were once your friends turn on you simply because you have been "accused." The accusations are overwhelming and intensely hurtful.

It does not happen often but from time to time we hear, read, or see a story of a man who has been incarcerated for a number of years; then to be let go because our judicial systems has determined these individuals did not perpetrate the crimes they were accused of. They are exonerated because of new tests or DNA diagnosis.

We all sit back and think this is so devastating. How these men were forced to endure these hardships for something they did not do. Why do I believe I can reach out to these men? I am hard pressed to find anyone outside of maybe therapists or counselors who are doing this. I have lived through it and seen first-hand the flaws in the system.

I want to offer you this hope; someone is out there who really understands and has experienced it. There really is a God out there, who sees everything and Oh how he loves you and wishes to set you free. I will say right now and will expound on it later;

NOTHING JUST HAPPENS!

<u>It is all for a purpose and will eventually be revealed!</u>

I can tell you with all I believe and know there was no one who has ever lived who suffered more than Jesus Christ. He experienced the ultimate when it comes to enduring abuse. He chose the abuse so we could be set free. Jesus was rejected by all mankind, yet He freely gave his life for all of us. Jesus exemplifies the very thing to combat abuse and abusive situations, LOVE!

Understanding exactly what is abuse, is a good place to start. So what is abuse? Just as each person has a definition of love, they also have a definition of abuse. It is a hard question for many to answer. Many people have a misunderstanding of what abuse is. This is why many people will suffer abuse and not realize exactly what abuse is. They live for years and always wonder why, "It's happening again."

I believe abuse is when you, as a person, are forced to do something against your will, or one is treated in an offensive way. It can be physical or mental. It may happen once or it could be ongoing. Abuse can be one large event, abuse can be smaller incidents strung together. While one large event may leave you feeling violated, sometimes those small violations add up to a lifestyle, which is unhealthy for everyone involved. Abuse can be physical and it can also be verbal. It can be experienced first party (directly), or second party (indirectly). More than not this often is the case with children.

It can happen anywhere. It can happen at any time. Abuse perpetrated against men often goes unreported and undetected. I believe a lot of this is due to this fact; over history men have been conditioned to accept a lot of things. I believe if men become aware of this then a lot of abuse, which is thrown onto women, can be alleviated.

In March 2007 Rebecca Bailey wrote an article to look into different types of spousal abuse, which included; physical, sexual, emotional, economic, financial, passive and spiritual abuse as they pertained to abuse received from a spouse, mostly men suffering the abuse. This article is posted on www.suite101.com.

"**Spousal abuse**" is defined as someone who is treated in a harmful, injurious or offensive way by their legal spouse or significant other. It includes physical, sexual, emotional, economic, passive and spiritual abuse. Spousal abuse is not only aimed toward women, but men suffer as much if not more than women from it. It is not easy to just get out of the abusive situation. If you are experiencing abuse, many times you are scared and don't always know how to get out. Social pressure keeps you in the relationship. Let's take a look and see how they affect every day life, as well as how to get out.

Physical abuse- Physical abuse is common in society today. Studies show not only are women the victims, even though it is not heard of a lot, there are also men who are victims of an abusive wife. We don't hear much about men being abused because many do not report it because it is socially unacceptable. Physical abuse is abuse involving contact intended to cause pain or other physical harm. The main indications of physical abuse are bruises or cuts on the skin from some type of force. These are often described by the victim as an accident.

Sexual abuse – Many intimate partners who are victims of sexual assault are often at risk of serious injury or death. Sexual harassment is an attempt by the abuser to gain power over another person; this often leads into sexual assault by rape. Sexual exploitation is a power trip forcing someone to look at pornography or forcing them to participate in pornographic film making. It is manipulating your spouse or others into performing sexual acts, which he or she is uncomfortable in doing.

Emotional abuse- Emotional abuse can be both verbal and nonverbal. This abuse is often believed to be worse than even physical abuse because the scars are deep rooted and cannot be seen. It has also been proven to be more emotionally damaging than physical abuse. Victims of emotional abuse are threatened or intimidated into compliance or submission. They have had their personal property or possessions destroyed or stolen. Society and media outlets over the past thirty to forty years have provided propaganda showing the main victims of emotional abuse are women. However, studies show men suffer as much if not more than women in these cases. Victims of emotional abuse become a possession of the abuser and are isolated from family and friends being made to feel worthless in life. (This was me to a T)

Economic or Financial abuse- Economic and financial abuse are part of the isolation process. The victim is often prevented from working or choosing an occupation. The abuser will often withhold money, credit cards, food, clothes, and necessary medication; as well as shelter from the victim to force submission. Stealing from or defrauding the victim of money or assets and exploitation of resources for personal gains also are signs of economic or financial abuse. This is perpetrated a lot upon the elderly or handicapped individual.

Spiritual abuse- Spiritual abuse is the acts of preventing the victim from practicing their religious or spiritual beliefs, as well as ridiculing them for these beliefs. Using these beliefs to manipulate the victim is another form of this abuse. You can also find the abuser often forces the victim to raise their children in a religion or spiritual preference other than the victims.

Now that you are aware of the types of abuse let's look at the signs you or a friend could be in an abusive relationship:

- Depression, irrational behavior, paranoia.
- Absences from work.

- Harassing phone calls while the victim is working.
- Fear of the partner. Fear of making decisions.
- Decreased productivity.
- Isolation.
- Insufficient resources

When your boss, a police officer, or someone else is in a position of authority over you, and they take advantage of their position, it often leaves you feeling violated; this is abuse. When abuse happens in your personal life, it becomes even more difficult to cope with. Abuse can escalate into the verbal, emotional, physical, or sexual realms. When abuse becomes a pattern, it almost seems impossible to move on.

Ask yourself this question, is the pattern part of your life, or do you see the pattern as life? Some will never realize yet alone be able to identify this. Some relationships have abusive episodes. A strike, a shove, a kick; because it is isolated does not make it acceptable. So what is the difference between an abusive episode and an abusive relationship?

Abusers always shift the blame, they never accept responsibility.

The differences concern frequency, consequences, and responsibility; it's about intentions. There are people who have a bad night, or a few bad episodes, but they learn from them. They aren't abusive. Despite the consequences, an abuser keeps abusing. They refuse to take responsibility, shifting blame for the abuse to the victim, and not themselves. Abusers are unable or accept self examination.

My ex-wife was raised in an abusive home. She claimed her father regularly beat her mother for years. She told me when her father tried to visit her sister one night when her sister was 16 to sleep with her, her mother stepped in between them and her father beat her mother to a pulp. She also claimed her father regularly sexually abused her as a child. Yet through my whole ordeal, she never once identified her father to be abusive, only me. It was easier to blame me and not her father.

All of this information came out when my wife began to visit a "spiritual counselor." I had no idea of any of this for the first 20 years of my marriage. She would take the children every summer to visit her family. If her father was such an abuser, then why would she continue to visit and potentially expose my children to the same abuse she would have received when she was a child?

It was this same "spiritual counselor" who led her and my children down a path to believe I had done the abusing, to her first, and then my children. I was the one to whom the blame was shifted. It is easier for a severely abused person to shift the blame to someone else instead of dealing with the pain and hurt. Even in the police report she stated this about her father, yet I was the one arrested. In fact more was reported in the police report about her father, than of me!

What concerned me the most was not only did she claim she was abused by her father, but my children started claiming the same things at the same time about their Grandfather. This in itself drew concern.

Where I began having problems with these stories and believing them was not only did they claim my wife's father was the perpetrator, but also stated her mother witnessed it and even gave approval. She also claimed my stepson, my father, my mother, my wife's brother, and a whole host of others were also perpetrators.

I tried talking to my wife about it and all I received was "how can you say this, and you're insensitive." It was at this point the counselor began talking them into believing I was to blame because of my "callous approach;" because I failed to believe his diagnosis and counseling.

Since I was falsely accused, it places in my mind a greater amount of uncertainty, whether or not my wife really ever was abused at all. Somewhere in the mix, as this spiritual advisor was trying to help her, I believe she began speaking about it to my children and they in turn began to live out my ex-wife's stories themselves. All their lives, my children were medically cared for. There was never any hint or any evidence of abuse; ever!

All my children's stories bear striking resemblances to my ex-wife's stories of her childhood abuse. Corresponding ages are the same and in some instances the very places and times of day are similar. Yet my children have always stated they never had or have had memories of abuse. They only claim anything when in the presence of this counselor. Once removed from him, they revert back to normalcy.

I know they are fabrications because I never did any of the things they are claiming. All subsequent charges against me were dropped. All of this coupled with the fact this "spiritual counselor" had them believing everyone but the family dog was abusing them!

I submitted myself to psychological sexual tests and professional polygraph examinations, all point to my innocence. It was all during this time my ex-wife made all sorts of other allegations against me. She claimed I physically hit her, but I never did. If I ever did do these things there would have been records.

She claims I admitted to having an affair. As time went on this accusation morphed into me having multiple affairs and having second and third families, which I was supporting around the United States.

She began speaking these sorts of stories after they were all informed of the psychological reports and polygraph results of my innocence. From the court room stand she began to speak these things. She also claimed under oath in a deposition, I made my children watch pornography and I watched pornography on my computer.

There were however, a number of occasions during our marriage when she struck me in the arms, face, and chest. Over our 25 year marriage she also had bitten me, kicked me, and threw objects at me and so on.

She also claimed I abused my children through discipline. No allegations like these over 25 yrs but on the stand the stories came forth. But she was the one who was always at home with them over our marriage as she homeschooled them.

Any and all physical discipline came through her. All her counseling from this spiritual advisor man came by way of "repressed memory therapy." All these memories were "assumed" to be repressed because they were so terrible, she forgot all of them. Yet she would remember the smallest details of things we spoke about 25 years in the past. She also remembered in graphic detail events of her first marriage.

We covered the subject of repressed memories thoroughly in my first book. However, even though all of her abuse knowledge came by way of these repressed memories it still translated to me into abuse. I became the abuse victim. She heaped all of her past hurt onto me. They then took all of their abused stories and tried to transfer them to me.

Another part of the psychological abuse came in the fact she would wake me up in the middle of the night. At first I did not know she was doing this. I remember always waking up in the middle of the night. Later in her testimony she admitted to doing this because she said "I was not breathing and did not want me to die."

In this form of abuse she then said I would get up in the middle of the night and leave the house. Yes I did get up only because she woke me up, and no I never left the house! Then her spiritual advisor told her and me on one of my visits that the reality of it was, I really deep down despised her because I had homosexual tendencies and in reality I could not sleep in the same bed with her...unreal!

She actually believed this stuff and it was her who woke me up at night to start!!! That's correct! She woke me up at night to get me to breath for years before she met her counselor. Then she believed her counselor, and put the blame onto me.

You see, ultimately abuse is about power and control. Her waking me up was about power and control. When Jesus was crucified it was about power and control. The religious authorities saw Jesus as a threat and had to have him removed. In their eyes the most secure way to solidify the control they wielded was to kill Jesus.

Whether it is rape, spousal abuse, child molestation, or psychological and other emotional abuse, it is about control and asserting power over another individual. The abusers get an adrenalin rush out of his or her control. They become addicted to it, they must possess it. They must abuse. It is as addictive as heroin or any other drug. They cannot do without it.

Controlling others is how an abuser controls his or her victim's lives. They use a variety of manipulation methods to obtain this control, but what it all amounts to is power and control. I fully believe when I challenged my wife's allegations stemming from the hands of her counselor and backed it up with solid scientific evidence; it became a situation of control and power on all of their parts. I believe with all of my heart this; if she could have killed me, she would have!

This did not set well with Marion Knox, her counselor. This counselor saw his beliefs and therapy threatened by me, he reacted in order to keep and assert his power and control over her. As time has gone by we have received dozens of emails asserting the same. As soon as we challenged this man, then the arrests and formal accusations started. In past episodes with this counselor, he became bent on wielding his sword of vindictiveness because we challenged him.

It appears the crux of Knox's involvement with many similar families encompassed a young female or mother. I have written testimony from other families who had daughters the same age as mine and Knox wielded his abusive power through them against their parents. All of the stories and testimonies end with the same outcome.

At my department of human services hearing concerning these allegations by the State of Oregon, my ex-wife began to say things out of her mind. On the stand she said during our 25 year marriage I had raped her on two occasions. She claimed both of these occasions resulted in her getting pregnant with my two sons. Now what person in their right mind would sit there and say to my children they were not wanted and were a product of rape and at the same time claim I was abusing my children?

Marion Knox has other females who claim he has helped them as well. They also claim their husbands beat them, raped them, and sodomized their children. They also claim their fathers sexually assaulted them, mainly by being sodomized.

Our marriage was good for 20 years. We were not a perfect family but we had love. Never once did terms like abuse, sodomy, or rape ever get mentioned.

Once she started seeing this counselor regularly without my knowledge everything changed. He began to abuse her psychologically, which in turn was pushed off to me. The world she knew ceased to exist and was replaced with the illusions this counselor parlayed into her mind. He sought to dominate her through power and control.

He portrayed himself into being a spokesman for God and some sort of an unapproachable savior who helped open her eyes to the truth. This I believe coupled with her fears and past hurts, "pushed her right over the edge of the cliff."

She began making the statement of abuse in our home. She claims I admitted to abusing my children in the presence of these counselors. This counselor under oath claimed I made no such comments I ever did abuse my children.

Living in an abusive relationship is life on a roller coaster. Abuse, like a roller coaster has a cycle or pattern within the individual relationship. For a time things seem to be okay, things get better, you have hope. Behind the scenes the tension is building the whole time; building, building, and then suddenly the decline hits. It only has the power to repeat because the victim permits it to. The roller coaster is a life being led by the engines and not the pilot.

The cycle or pattern repeats over and over, the good times are fewer, the buildups are shorter, and the abusive episodes escalate. Just like the roller coaster, only this one doesn't end when the ride is over, it just keeps going, up and down and all around. The roller coaster keeps repeating the cycle, faster and faster it goes until it carries off the track. The engine keeps running faster and faster because the pilot (you) is not in control.

In the next chapters I want to share what I believe is the cause of abuse and what I believe is the foundation for abuse. I want to challenge men to examine their lives for the signs of abuse. For many, you will discover you are a victim of abuse and may not even realize it.

In order for you to be free as a victim of abuse you have to first recognize there are abuses and what person it is, which the abuser is, and which one is the abused. You have to take control and quit relying on the engines or external forces.

To move from victim to survivor you have to be able "to call a spade a spade." In my research for this book and studying my personal log, I realized I in fact was suffering from abuse and did not even know it or realize it.

As I have said, abuse really is about power and control. The abuser in reality is having a temper tantrum and is demanding something from the abused. Unless those who are being abused stand up to it and are willing to challenge and confront it, it will go unchanged. It has been proven and we have all seen how a person abused goes back to or enter into another abusive relationship. This happens if the abused leave under any circumstances other than by their own free choice. Sometimes this is not even good enough.

It takes more than a 12 step program or extensive counseling. I believe only the Lord Jesus Christ can truly set someone free. Only he possesses the power to set the captive free. Those keys were given to him when he freely chose to die on the cross for yours and my sin.

You see Jesus was not only abused, He chose to be abused so you and I could be free. That is why He is the only one who can set you free, because He chose the abuse. Jesus freely accepted it. My prayer is your eyes are opened to recognize, which type of abuse is evident in your lives. I pray you truly experience salvation through the blood of Jesus. If you have never known him, then please bow your head and read this prayer.

Dear Jesus. I ask you to come into my heart. Be my Lord and Savior. Set me free from abuse and my abusive situation. I believe you died and shed your blood for me on the cross so that I can be free and forgiven. I believe your shed blood sets me free. I ask you to come into my heart. I give you my life unconditionally. In Jesus name I pray, Amen!

If you have prayed this prayer, then you are well on your way to possessing a new life. I will not promise you it will be easy and free of incident. But, you have taken the first step of many toward a new life and freedom. Find a bible and read the Gospel of John. Find a good bible believing church. I have provided contact information at the end of this book. Contact me and I will help you find a good place to garner support for your situation.

Just like the Wright brothers, you have to believe you are in control of your airplane, you and only you. You have lived through your experiences. You know them best. It is not in the external forces or engines, but it is within you to discover and stand firm, you are in control.

<u>No one else, only you.</u>

Notes Chapter 2

[1] http://standyourground.com/forums/index.php?topic=3482.0;wap2

[2] "The Wright Brothers & the Invention of the Aerial Age," *Smithsonian Institution.*

[3]   Padfield, Gareth D., Professor of Aerospace Engineering, and Ben Lawrence, researcher. "The Birth of Flight Control: An Engineering Analysis of the Wright Brothers' 1902 Glider." (PDF format) *The Aeronautical Journal,* Department of Engineering, The University of Liverpool, UK, December 2003.

<u>Chapter Three</u>
Face Your Fears

"You must face your fear! We cannot conquer what we are not willing to confront & we cannot confront what we are not willing to acknowledge exists!" – Stephan Skotko

I was really encouraged when I began my quest to publish my first book as to what professionals claimed were key ingredients to pass from being a victim to a survivor. I thank God for sending my psychiatrist into my life. She began to explain to me how I was going through a period of mourning and experiencing grief. She encouraged me to share with others my grief. She encouraged me to be open with her. She took the time to explain to me what mourning is all about. How we need grieving process as part of our healing, and how we suffer adversely if it is removed or ended prematurely from our lives.

When I began to share my thoughts and offer encouragement to others, I was amazed how much certain therapists did not know or understand about their patients. I was amazed how many were given drugs too soon and not permitted to live out his or her grieving process. God began to open up to me a new world into how people act, react, and function in society. I learned just how many people are prescribed medication, which they may not need.

All of those other therapists I speak of are good people who had not witnessed or experienced abuse except through much trial and error with their patients. I want to offer it through my eyes; the eyes of a victim become a survivor. I am not an expert or offer any medical advice, but I am well on the road to becoming a "Victor," one who is triumphantly traversing this threshold to a healing in my life.

I have spent a lot of time over the years developing my personal beliefs and devotion as a Christian. I firmly believe pain is a masterful tool in the hands of God to reach us. I have read the bible numerous times since graduating from high school. I know first-hand the powerful and remarkable results, which come by way of pain.

I remind myself of a story found in the book of Judges in the old testament of the bible. Gideon was a man who had to face his fear. Judges chapter 6 gives the story of an encounter, which would change Gideon's life forever.

The story begins with an Angel of the Lord visiting Gideon while he is sifting wheat in a wine press. The reason he is in the wine press is because he was hiding from the Midianites (the people who abused the children of Israel for seven years during a time where it is recorded the children of Israel were disobedient). The angel calls Gideon a "Mighty Man of Valor" ("noble", "virtue", "brave").

The angel instructed Gideon to tear down the altar of Baal and build an altar to the LORD – (v.26). In Gideon's world the altars of Baal were a picture of his fear. Fear was what Gideon needed to confront in contrary to what many theologians believe were simply the Midianites themselves to be victorious in his life and for his people.

The armies and people of Midian were simply the mask, which fear adorned. In recovering and transforming yourself from being a victim, you will have to defeat fear in your life, and not the object (mask), which is being adorned by Fear. The object or (mask) is often pain associated with the fear.

After Gideon is convinced it was God calling him, he follows through on God's command and destroys the altar of Baal (fear). The Midianites worshipped the god "Baal. Baʿal, (bāʾ-ʿayn-lām), is a Semitic word signifying "A male lord, master, owner, keeper, or husband". Baal is the one who was in control.

Since the Midianites controlled Israel they were able to erect altars to their god "Baal" in the Land of Israel. By submitting to the Midianites the Israelites literally permitted the beliefs of the Midianites to permeate their land, in essence, their lives. The Midianites inflicted pain on Israel. This pain caused their fear.

When confronted by his countrymen after tearing down the altars of baal, Gideon tells them "the Lord commanded us to worship Him and Him alone". The moment Gideon faced his fear and tore it down, was the moment God began the process of delivering His people from bondage (Their fears). Gideon's pain finally drew Gideon to a place where he was able to "call a spade a spade," recognize the "devil for who he was."

It was also a time in Gideon's life, in which he went from victim to survivor and then to victor or leader. As a matter of fact, Gideon was so convinced God was with him he built an altar to the Lord and called it – The-LORD-Is-Peace (v.24).Gideon replaced his fear with faith.

<u>Faith is the ability to see the outcome without any evidence</u>.

No matter what your religious persuasion or belief you can glean a lot of insight from this passage from the bible. We are all mighty people. Each and every one of us is a mighty, unique individual. When my hearing was finished in March of 2009 there was such a relief. I remember standing outside the Linn county courthouse in Albany, Oregon. My attorney looked at me and with a big smile on his face said,

"Steve you won! You won't ever have to face these charges again."

I had won. I was so relieved, I just stood there stunned. My mother who had traveled to Oregon for the hearing touched my arm and just smiled. It was as if Niagara Falls was in my head. The flood of tears just let loose and I just began to weep.

The ceiling of today's victories become the floor for the next battle.

I was so stunned, I just began to weep and cry. I remember thinking at this moment it was over. Little did I know it was not over! What appeared to be a great victory, and it was, was not quite over. Still looming in front of me was the raging beast wanting to devour me. The whole ordeal is an obstacle course. I had just graduated up to the next level. It was now time to lay the battle plans for the next encounter.

It was not much later when I realized the greatest battle was to be fought. It was the long drawn out war, in which I would engage the true enemy, known as Fear. I began to realize how big Fear was in my life, how big of a rival it was and had grown to be, and the power it possessed to attempt to destroy my life.

I would have to face my Fear and conquer it. We not only heal and recover when we face our fears, but our decisions always influence others in the same way. Many at this point give up thinking there is no more to deal with. When you do this, they the enemy will overrun your life.

What is even more amazing about this story of Gideon was the children of Israel were living in their own country. This was the Promised Land, which God had promised He would give to them.

This would be like you the reader, living in your home for years and years. You are comfortable. You have established yourself there. You have done the decorating, painting, fixed the broken fence in the yard. You have landscaped your yard, planted trees and shrubs, put in a new sidewalk. The property is yours.

To make it even more of a feel good story, the house, land, and everything else has been given to you. It was a gift so to say from a relative. Actually it was first given to your grandfather, and has been passed down to your father and then to you.

You are happy dwelling there. All your needs are met. The well provides you with water. Animals are numerous. You can hunt, fish, and farm your land at your own leisure.

Then one day a stranger moves on your land. They begin telling you what to do. You try to stand up to them, but they kill your animals, kidnap your kids, and then they kill your family. You are stunned. You cannot believe it. You are terrified. You can't call the police, because they have done the same thing to them. The police have been bribed to support the enemy.

This enemy has taken control of the whole land. They are everywhere. Then the enemy forces you out of your house and you are reduced to living in caves and under trees.

This is what it was like in the days of Gideon. The Israelites were totally and completely overwhelmed by the enemy. They had settled in and thought the war was over. They had won many battles; but they quit prematurely.

There was total fear, which permeated the land. The Israelites were powerless. They were powerless in the own land, in their own homes. Then they rose up and confronted the enemy, the Fear. All the while they had the power, the manpower, and the resources to win. They just did not know they had it.

Not only do we have the power to confront our fears and conquer them, but we also have the power and ability to "tear them down" forever. We have the ability to dramatically change our negative circumstances, which bring fear into our lives.

You are their miracle.

When we act upon and tear down our fears and replace them with new ideas and goals, there is always someone else who will draw strength, power, and encouragement. Not only will you win, but others, some of whom you do not know, will benefit from you conquering your Fear. You are their miracle, you just don't know it. None of this will happen unless you face your fears and overcome them.

After I won the hearing and when confronted with my circumstances, the first thing I had to overcome was Fear. Even though all the allegations were totally false about me the fact still remained the majority of those in my life believed they were true or took no stance. In both cases I was isolated and alone. In both cases I wound up garnering very little support overall. I had more against me than for me.

The largest obstacle, which associated itself with fear in my life, was the power in the accusation itself. It was "fear" from and of the accusation.

I experienced first-hand the effects of those accusations.

Accusations were the altar, which fear was able to erect in my life (land). I was afraid to be alone with women, children, or those at a disadvantage in life not because of something I would do, but because of the power and the bite of the accusation.

Those accusations literally scared me stiff. To combat one's own fear, it is human tendency to accuse others, regardless of guilt or innocence. In reality the accuser (fear) accused me because of the accusers own fears in their life.

The Power of the accusation

In 1692, a group of young Puritan girls who lived in the small New England village of Salem, Massachusetts accused dozens of people of witchcraft, or channeling with the devil. In studies of the Salem Witch Trials, along with other events in American history, historians have searched, time and time again, for answers to this probing question: What secret motivations or reasons lie behind the accusations of the innocent? What drives individuals to fabricate stories, which may destroy the lives, marriages, and livelihood of those he or she is accusing?

In the Salem Witch Trials, the accusations were clearly caused by the girls' own fears, and the fears of the community also led to the use of scapegoats for the evils of Salem. From this point in American history forward, dozens upon dozens of innocent people were burned alive simply because they were "accused" of being a witch. The accusers fear gave fuel to their propaganda. Their fear literally transferred itself to those who were accused. It was mass hysteria!

Arthur Miller, who wrote The Crucible, a play depicting the tragic events, which occurred in Salem, was "profoundly, angrily concerned with the immediate issues of our society." Miller lived during the 1950s, an era renowned for the philosophy of McCarthyism; a great paranoia and fear of the spread of Communism.

Miller wrote the following taken from the Crucible.

"Persons who scoffed at accusations of witchcraft risked becoming targets of accusations themselves. One man who was openly critical of the trials paid for his skepticism with his life."

John Proctor, a central figure in Arthur Miller's fictionalized account of the Salem witch hunt was an opinionated tavern owner who openly denounced the witch hunt.

Testifying against Proctor were Ann Putnam, Abigail Williams, Indian John (a slave of Samuel Parris who worked in a competing tavern), and eighteen-year-old Elizabeth Booth, who testified ghosts had come to her and accused Proctor of serial murder.

Proctor fought back, accusing confessed witches of lying, complaining of torture, and demanding that his trial be moved to Boston. The efforts proved futile. Proctor was hanged. His wife Elizabeth, who was also convicted of witchcraft, was spared execution because of her pregnancy (reprieved "for the belly").

No execution caused more unease in Salem than of the village's ex-minister, George Burroughs. Burroughs, who was living in Maine in 1692, was identified by several of his accusers as the ringleader of the witches. Ann Putnam claimed that Burroughs bewitched soldiers during a failed military campaign against Wabanakis in 1688-89, the first of a string of military disasters, which could be blamed on an Indian-Devil alliance.

In her interesting book, *In the Devil's Snare*, historian Mary Beth Norton argues, the large number of accusations against Burroughs, and his linkage to the frontier war, is the key to understanding the Salem trials. Norton contends the enthusiasm of the Salem court in prosecuting the witchcraft cases owed in no small measure to the judges' desire to

"Shift the blame for his or her inadequate defense of the frontier."
Many of the judges, Norton points out, played lead roles in a war effort, which had been markedly unsuccessful.

During the 1950s, hundreds of innocent people were accused of being Communists plotting to overthrow the government of the United States. This anger with the events, which transpired during the middle of twentieth century, was what motivated Miller to write The Crucible [1].

Those who accuse are in the same boat as those who abuse. It's all about power and control over those they perceive are weaker.

Personally speaking many people cruised in and out of my life during the time I was thrust into my War. Many offered help and encouragement, but the fact remained I began this journey nearly alone.

Most if not all of my former "friends" believed the accusations and metaphorically, "burned me at the stake." This was the basis for my fear. It started in the abandonment by others of me over the years while living in an abusive or toxic relationship with my ex-wife.

It was fueled because of the power in the accusation. Except for a chosen few (and I mean two or three) even those who confessed their support always held in the back of their minds "the what if" opinion. It makes me wonder if indeed they were really friends at all.

Because my ex-wife coveted fear in her life; eventually her fear became my fear. She failed to deal with it so an altar of fear (accusation) was erected in my life. Her fear grew because of resentment from her past. This caused my fear.

Tearing down your altars will always inflict some pain on others

My fear permitted the accusations to take hold in my life, or in "my land," it began to erect altars. I literally had to tear down those altars to be free from the fear, which permeated my life (land). This is why my friend two years ago told me to "let it go, it is too big for your shoulders to carry."

Tearing down those altars is a painful experience. Some I have met would rather leave them there and have a half hearted relationship, than to painfully tear them down and have a permanent strong relationship. In dealing with other families ripped apart like my own, many of them won't confront or tear down the altars because it will cause their children pain. But the pain is the only thing, which will set their children free.

What is interesting about this description is those few people who were totally behind me are also the only ones who flat out asked me, "Did you do it and are you guilty." All the others never did. I never resented the fact they asked me the question. I am glad they did.

However, they were my friends and they believed me when I answered them. There are still times even after three years where I experience moments and feel totally isolated. During these moments when left by myself I have to deal one on one with my thoughts and prayers. In these times I am totally and completely exhausted.

Bill Cornelius writes in his book, "I dare you to change" the following, which really hit home for me.

Page 97, "Once you start pursuing your goals, you will face obstacles. One of the biggest challenges will be exhaustion. You may become discouraged and find yourself tempted to quit. The book of Galatians tells us,

__'Let us not become weary in doing well, for at the proper time we will__
__reap a harvest if we do not give up' Galatians 6:9__

*God assumes when you are doing well you will get extremely tired. But
tiredness and exhaustion and thoughts of giving up are part of the price
you pay for the harvest. In fact, one of the signs that you are near the
harvest is that feeling of exhaustion. Therefore, being tired should not
make you quit. Instead, it should make you double your efforts. When
you are tired it is often a sign that you are close to reaching your goal."*

Bill's book, "I dare you to change" is based upon the Life of
Gideon, located in the Old Testament in the book of Judges. I had
already had the foundation for this chapter before the publication of his
book. Reading his book brought me great encouragement and
confirmation to my manuscript.

Just when I would feel I was not going to survive, God would
always and faithfully, send someone with an "olive branch" to bring
encouragement or a consoling word. This is all a part of the healing
process, which is a time to erect the new altars in my life in the absence
of all the old fears.

This is a difficult time for anyone who is experiencing this. It is
often during this time when many are simply grieving. In my opinion,
many health professionals over the years have misdiagnosed this
grieving for depression.

**Many people at this critical intersection of their lives are "carried
off on a rabbit trail," of depression. Right away doctors and others
put them on medication, which I personally believe stops their
grieving process and freezes their healing and transition.**

My psychiatrist explained this to me in detail. I remember sitting there in her office. No matter how strong I tried to be and not cry, the floodgates would open and I began weeping. I asked her if she thought I was depressed. She told me no. She told me I was grieving and to give it time to pass. If it did not over a period of time then she would recommend I be put on some medication.

"What we are not willing to confront we cannot and will not conquer! What we do not conquer in our life will eventually consume our thoughts and eventually devour us, hence, kill us."

Think of an area of your life, which is unfruitful or unproductive. You may be falsely accused of crimes or things you did not do.

I received a testimony from an individual who had read my first book. I was in Pueblo, Colorado, in the autumn of 2011 visiting my friend Pastor Darin Carroll. On the last night I was there he asked me to speak at a Wednesday night gathering. This person was in attendance on this night. This is her testimony.

Dear Steve here is my testimony,

All my life I have struggled with bi polar disorder and I realize a lot of times it's because the brain is doing something wrong, (IDK, "I don't know. LOL, "Laugh out loud"). However, God showed me a long time ago it was not physical it was something spiritual and emotional.

Despite seeking help over and over again, and being on anti-depressants, it would not leave my life and I was unchanged. Over time

I just gave up (about 15 years now). I just stayed on my medication and did my best to function but it has always broken my heart because I have not been as close to God because of this at least I felt I have not.

Anyways, when I picked up your book something strange happened, that thing started to manifest, well it scared me and I could not figure out what was going on so I put down the book and stopped reading it.

Wednesday night when you were praying for people it happened again and of course the kids started acting up and we had to leave the service.

4am Thursday morning God showed me what the thing was and I now realize why it manifested around you and when I tried to read your book. It is because you were exposing it.

This is very hard for me because I have buried this thing so deep I never wanted to deal with it again but here it is. When my sister was 11 and I was 12 years old (not sure if you remember this incident) we were kidnapped by a woman from our parents.

This woman was not a counselor but she I believe was a witch and she would do strange things to us and others. What happened to your wife, happened to me, we were brain washed.

Slowly I became this other person. I became callous. I remember watching my sister get beat and laugh. Slowly, I came to get these memories (whew this is tough lol) of my Dad doing things to me that I felt never happened but it was so real to me that I did report him and caused all kinds of trouble in our family.

Our parents got us back after about 6 months and over the years my sister and I felt as if we had recovered (or so I thought). We swore an oath to each other to never speak of it again and so I buried it and it was this thing God exposed fully.

 I battled it for 2 days after he showed me and I feel it pretty much left. Then I began to not be able to handle Bi-polar medication. The doctor confirmed this and is slowly taking me off of the medication and I do feel I am being healed

Thank you God!! The only thing is I think there are things I do not understand about it so that I can be fully rid of it. Maybe you can help me in that area but I believe it is fully exposed and losing power. I feel that already. THANK YOU JESUS!!! Ok that's it and that's the first I have talked about it. No one else even knows about any of this, besides our family of course. Thank you again and whatever you have to share to help would be greatly appreciated."

Maybe you are in jail, maybe you are not. You have been cut off from what you once called your life. Circumstances have changed for you. Sadly, many turn inward and fill their lives with alcohol and drugs.

Many figure "what is the use" and just choose to throw every hope, every dream away. Maybe your fear is of yourself. Who knows you better than yourself? You fear the things you once did. You fear what you may do again. In essence you have not fully recovered from your fear. What you are doing is hiding in the winepress of life!

Chances are you know what needs to be done to make your life fruitful and productive again. Just like this individual, you know what you have to do. You just need to face the fears and engage them in battle. Maybe you are in a strained marriage, maybe it's out of control spending, or maybe it's a hostile work environment.

Listen, the longer you ignore your problem the worse it will get. It got so bad for Gideon he resorted to hiding in a well, a winepress! Don't be like a lot of others who avoid the window, instead pull back the curtain, face your fears, and you will see the only thing causing fear is a little wind blowing in your life and the last I heard a little wind never hurt anyone!

The Steve Skotko bandwagon, low self esteem

Along with the fear I was battling in my life, was the fact I was also dealing with a horrible bout of low self esteem. I felt like a total failure. It was surreal. My wife and children turned against me. Their minds were polluted by the hands of this weirdo and his screwed up therapy, in the name of religion. They still are today.

Not only was my family deceived, but friends, business associates, and others turned against me. It was the popular thing in Albany, Oregon to ride on the Steve Skotko band wagon, and the band was playing very loud. It was like everyone got in line to ride the train. It looked like a scene from a movie where there are hundreds of people draped over and on a single small vehicle! That is the way it felt.

My life was a nightmare. One of those weird dreams you have so when you wake up, you lie there and just think, "What was that all about?" I discovered many things about myself and what Steve was all about. I saw beneath everyone's mask as they tore them off. In my quest for answers and information, a person I have never met sent me the following letter by way of 'email' at a most opportune time.

.

"Dear Stephan,
Here is an article you may find informative:
Low Self Esteem - How Psychologically Abusive Relationships Impact
Our Self Perception.

Low self esteem is an affliction, which impacts a large number of
people at some point in their lives. It causes beautiful, successful,
intelligent people to doubt their self worth and purpose for being. It
prevents individuals from reaching the true heights of their potential,
and worst of all, keeps many in a state of depression and sadness, which
is unshakeable.

Our relationships can either support or lower our self esteem. Sadly, for
many with low self esteem, their relationships can cause a negative
snowballing effect. Those who don't value themselves tend to attract
and be attracted to those who will not treat them with respect and love.
Some of these relationships are outright abusive.

The underlying problem with such negative relationships is there is
programming occurring. A person who is psychologically abusive has
an agenda, and part of that agenda is controlling the other partner.
Already suffering from low self esteem, the non-abusive partner is a
prime candidate for the emotional and mental manipulation handed out
by the abusive partner.

An abuser seeks to create a reality and a perception by the other partner,
which removes resistance to their agenda of control. Thus, an abuser
will do what he or she can to undermine the other's sense of their own
judgment, skill, and even moral decency. Without good self esteem, the

abused partner assimilates this programming, further diminishing his or her feelings of self worth.

The cure for the negative effects of such a psychologically abusive relationship is removal from the source. While self esteem is created and rebuilt, all negative influences must be removed. To conjure an image to illustrate the point, before a dam can hold back the water again, the holes must be repaired and filled.

The strength to follow through with a period of reduced, or no contact can be increased through reprogramming the false set of beliefs the abuser has pushed upon you. One of the most important methods of reprogramming yourself is to spend time with and around the people in your life who are trustworthy, kind, and concerned for your well being above all else. It is likely the stronger and more positive your sense of self becomes, the less you will desire contact with which person you have been psychologically abused.

I hope this was helpful to you.
All the Best
Shannon Cook"

I personally do not know Shannon. I found some of her writing on the internet when I was conducting research for my first book. I had sent her a personal 'email' to ask her if she would be so kind as to read the newspaper article, which was published in the Albany Democrat Herald on January 4, 2011.She then started sending me links to other writing on the net.

This was the first I believe, where she took an interest in my situation. It has been things like this, which have kept me focused and continuing on my path to recovery and being a survivor. Although I realize this was an article she had previously written; she put it into a form, which made it feel personal. I believe it was personal.

It is difficult, I can imagine; responding to everyone who contacts you and asks for advice or help. For me, I will take this and run. It was for me; I received it when I was experiencing an extremely low point along the path and it has helped me insurmountably. I read it over and over and it was so right on the money for me and my life.

Reality begins to hit home

The first thing I had to come to grips with and accept after reading this letter was my ex-wife ended our 25 year marriage where I was psychologically abused. I never thought of it while I was in it. Believe me I was not perfect and threw a bit of the psychological abuse back in the other direction from time to time out of anger.

In this thought I want to explain; I really don't even believe she realized consciously she was doing it to me most of the time. I always knew she was carrying a lot of hurt from her past marriage and her childhood. I also knew there were unsettled issues in my life I was carrying around with me. I believe this mix came to its head when she began receiving her "spiritual counseling" from Marion Knox.

I believe he lit the psychological fuse, which eventually detonated our lives. (If you are saying, "who is Marion Knox," then you will have to buy the first book "A Heart Held Ransomed," and read all about it. I believe the real root of the dandelion in our lives was "hurt."

Notes Chapter 3

[1] www.history.com/UnitedStates

<u>Chapter Four</u>
The Real Pieces create the Real "Peace"

"Life belongs to the living and he who lives must be prepared for changes"-Johann Von Goethe

I chose the title of this book, "Picking up the Pieces," because this was the way my life felt in 2008. My life was a giant jigsaw puzzle thrown about before me on the floor. I then realized the following. "You never know how strong you are until being strong is your only choice."

There it laid, thousands of pieces with no organization, meaning, and no structure. All the pieces of my life; thoughts, memories, dreams, achievements, failures, it was all there prostrate in a scattered mess. So I began reading. I was sitting on the bed of the small extended stay hotel room I was living in thinking about my life. I began looking up items of interest; this all led me to find information concerning puzzles.

I learned the first jigsaw puzzle was created around 1760, when John Spilsbury, a British engraver and mapmaker, mounted a map on a sheet of wood. He then sawed around each individual country.

Spilsbury used the product to aid in teaching geography. After catching on with the wider public, this remained the primary use of jigsaw puzzles until about 1820. Of all things, I thought, it was a map!

By the early 20th century, magazines and newspapers found they could increase their daily subscriptions by publishing puzzle contests. From pictures, puzzles then developed into other sorts of strategy solving contests. All of this began to make sense to me. I discovered puzzles may also include letters, numbers, shapes, and riddles.

A broken puzzle is basically an unsolved problem [1]. Yep, this was me; the map of my life had been shattered into thousands of pieces. I quickly realized I had a problem, and I needed to solve it.

Soren Kierkegaard said,

<u>"Life can only be understood backwards;</u>
<u>Unfortunately it can only be lived forward."</u>

In looking backward I can clearly see why my life resulted in the way it did. I now understand I had a huge problem and the puzzle of my life had no instructions to follow; there was no pretty picture on the cover. In just the past 2 months I had been removed from my home, estranged from my children, arrested, lost my vehicle, and my whole livelihood was gone.

I had to continue to live my life forward, no matter what outcome the past created. The world was not going to stop because my life was a mess. The world was not going to wait for Steve to catch up to it. The great maker of my puzzle left it for me to put together, or maybe I was left with the results of a lifelong regimen of bad decisions?

I did not even have enough money to quit

The first thing I did was stop. I began to assess my life. It is still ongoing today and will continue the rest of my life. I knew I faced an enormous task to begin to attempt to solve this problem. The thought was staggering. If not for my friend Gale, I would have quit. I could quit, I thought. Quitting would be easy. I could simply slam my life with drugs or alcohol and attempt to just forget about the whole thing, but I could not afford it, or I could somehow try come up with a plan to conquer my problem. It took me weeks to figure this out.

The amount of stress I was under was colossal. My body was racked with pain. I would wake up at night with cold sweats. This went on for about the first year. I had nightmares, day-mares, I needed support. The first thing I did was repair damaged relationships. I contacted both family and friends whom I had offended.

These relationships were severely damaged as a direct result of my situation and the abusive atmosphere, which I was no longer a part of. I knew I needed to create a support system in my life. I did not set out with the thought of "I need to build a support system," but, I wanted to set things right, which I had wronged. It did not matter if I thought I was to blame or not. I wanted to reconcile.

I would lie awake at night and see people's faces. Those faces consisted of family, friends, business acquaintances, my children, and people I had not seen in a lot of years. These were people who I offended at one time and people who had offended me. I wanted to correct any offenses, which existed. It was a lonely period of time.

It is this system of repaired relationships, which now supports me physically, emotionally, and spiritually. It makes you aware you're part of a bigger whole toward, which you also have a responsibility.

This will be the type of system, which will support you in times of need

Over the past four years I have learned the amount of strategy, which went into my ex-wife's decisions to end our relationship. Those decisions in no part were formulated completely by her. Premeditation is performed by someone or a collaboration of a group who knows exactly what they want to accomplish.

Support networks are extremely important when you're under stress. One of the problems caused by stress is tunnel vision. Tunnel vision is the inability to look at alternatives and options. This is where the term "I was so angry I could not see straight" comes from; straight not meaning a straight line, but viewing everything clearly and being able to assess the entire landscape of the situation.

Literally when you are controlled by stress and anger as a result of your situation your mind becomes focused and narrow. Your peripheral vision becomes non-existant. Also in comparison, when you are driven by fear you also lose your peripheral vision and tend to view things through a tube or tunnel. Even though you appear to be looking straight, the vision is not consistent; you cannot see the entire landscape. You cannot see the bigger picture!

A good simple example is getting angry and frustrated when you can't find your car keys. Oh man you stomp around; your angry, mad, and you literally can't see them. You are looking through a tunnel or tube and can only see directly in front of you.

Your anger controls your vision; it keeps it focused and transfixed, and you cannot see anything on the periphery. This is always at a time when you are in a hurry and under stress to get somewhere.

Then someone says "here they are" and all the while they were literally right near you. Just outside of your "narrowed, stressed filled eyesight." You just could not see them. Your periphery was diminished.

Stress also makes you feel paranoid. You feel people are trying to get you or they're purposely being difficult just to aggravate you. Your vision of your self is centered on you.

Your self esteem is low. You feel others are teaming up against you. Something small happens and right away you stop and say to yourself "what did I do, what did I say, I wonder if." when all the while the others decisions has nothing to do with you at all. You were the furthest thing from their mind!

My suggestion is to share your problem perception. Share it with the important people you have surrounded yourself with to see if you perceive things clearly. If they are close to you, then listen to them and have faith in your relationship with them. If there is no one there for you, then go and repair the damaged relationships in your life. Believe me they are there. This is what plague's me to this day. This is a huge obstacle course for me to navigate through in my life.

What's the problem?

A problem is defined as "an obstacle which hinders the achievement of a particular goal, objective, or purpose." It refers to a situation, condition, or issue, which is yet unresolved. In a broad sense, a problem exists when an individual becomes aware of a significant difference between what actually is and what is desired.

I was this individual. I wanted to learn why everything happened. I slowly, over time, broke down my problem in an attempt to solve it. Once I did this there was no going back. I had to rebuild. In essence, I figured out what the pieces of my puzzle represented in my life.

Looking back, I believe the main foundation of my life was solid. The problem is along the way I built additions on my life. Those additions were laid wrong. I watched over the next year as God removed those incorrect additions in my life. He removed them totally, foundation and all. He now is able to build a correct foundation for my life. This new foundation will carry me through. I am excited about the blueprints!

When you are made aware of the problem you are encountering then you have to be brave enough to accept the outcome and persevere to achieve the solution. Once you realize the problem you become accountable to resolve it. I could not do it on my own.

In my case, I had to trust in my God to bring me through it all. This is no small task! The solution will never ever change if we stick our head in the sand. The problem never goes away. In fact the longer we wait the deeper its roots get. The journey is painful, but I know I will make it through, as you will also.

Exercising your resources

A puzzle is also "an enigma, which tests the cleverness, resourcefulness, and ingenuity of the solver." Not only is an enigma a puzzle or riddle, it is also a mystery.

So I also discovered I had a mystery as well. Yes, the mystery's plot thickens every day I live; but, my resources to combat it also are made amply ready to defeat it and solve the mystery. With the processes during this time, my situation was a total mystery; not only to me, but also to those who have supported me.

Ingenuity refers to "the process of applying ideas to solve problems or meet challenges as defined scientifically." In a basic jigsaw puzzle, one is intended to put together pieces in a logical way to come up with the desired solution.

Today we know puzzles to be pictures. Puzzles are often contrived as a form of entertainment, but they can also stem from serious mathematical or logistical problems; in such cases, their successful resolution can be a significant contribution to mathematical research [2].

Solutions to puzzles may require recognizing patterns and creating a particular order. Hence, I have discovered an enormous amount of patterns, which have transpired in my lifetime. I have discovered patterns in my own life, which caused my dilemma.

I am sure everyone who has chosen to read this book has at one time or another constructed a puzzle. You have probably done so with your children or maybe adults gather in a time of friendship to put the puzzle together.

The usual strategy for a puzzle is to put the outside border together and then fill in the center. This is a good strategy and as you do the constructing you have a picture of the puzzle you are attempting to solve.

The puzzle of my life did not have a border, and the picture was unknown because most of the images on the pieces were gone. At the time I did not even know the images had disappeared. As time went by I discovered the images indeed had disappeared. When you add in the stress and abuse, which was present causing the limited vision, it was nearly impossible to even attempt to begin solving the puzzle.

Abuse coupled with pre-existing fear of the abused, and seasoned with stress magnifies everything. Words and gestures get misconstrued, misquoted, and misunderstood, especially when one is under a large amount of stress resulting from psychological abuse.

Abuse and fear stems from hurt.

When you pent up your hurt, mark it down, one day it will come forth as anger and usually at the wrong times. These times we term abusive. Abuse stems from pent up anger, which emanates from the hurt experienced in our lives. Anger is the fuel, which abuse uses to propel it forward. Just like motor fuel can propel the vehicle or can be ignited by itself; anger is refined from a person being hurt.

Ultimately we have the absolute power over our lives to keep from abusing someone, to keep from hurting them, even though you are hurt and angry. My own hurt and the things, which hurt me during my life, did not help matters along the way in my home prior to the devastation.

It is O.k. to get angry; it is not O.k. to be abusive.

No one under any circumstance deserves to feel disregarded, insulted, controlled, coerced, intimidated, hurt, hit, pushed, grabbed, or touched in any undesired or inappropriate way by you or anyone else. Nothing anyone says or does justifies abuse; also, one abuse never justifies another. [3] This is what my puzzle consisted of.

Anger is almost always a reaction to hurt. More often than not anger is a reaction to a threat of psychological hurt. Vulnerability to psychological hurt depends entirely on how we feel about ourselves.

Again the issue with our self-esteem arises. Low self-esteem or a diminished sense of self causes the reaction of anger in most cases.

Regaining our self worth or esteem will diminish anger and abusive actions towards others [3].

Psychological abuse chisels away at a person's self esteem and worth. Normally we don't realize we are being psychologically abused until we abuse someone else. Sad to say this always seems to be someone we really love. This hurts them and us deeply.

This is how the cycle of abuse exists in homes and families. Alarmingly, it goes on for generations. For example Mommy was married to an alcoholic. Daddy beat Mommy and the children. The children hate and resent Daddy for what he does to everyone. The children vow they will leave and never come back and never be a part of this type of situation again forever. Then the children get married. In most cases it is to an abusive alcoholic spouse. The cycle continues to the 3rd generation and so forth. People deal with the flower and not the root.

I remember when I was a child and I am talking really young. My mother would tell me to go pick all the dandelion heads on the front lawn of my home. I would go with my brown bag in hand and pick all those heads and then she would give me a nickel for my good work. She was We all know this action does not kill the dandelions because the root is still in the ground. However, it gave me a satisfaction of accomplishment and the praise of my mother, but the dandelions came roaring back a few days later.

This is the cycle of abuse. We feel better for a while because we deal with the head, or the flower. Because it looks like it is gone does not mean it is! The front lawn of our lives looks and feels great for a few days, but we fail to deal with the real issue, which is the hurt; the hurt is the root of the weed in our lives. Just ponder how much time you have spent "picking the heads" and not dealing with the real issues.

Here is another thought. Many of us mow the lawns of our lives. We know they are full of weeds, but we mow it to keep it under control. Once we are finished mowing, all the dandelion heads are gone. We think somehow they are, but the root is still in the ground. Some really believe the dandelions will go away after we mow or on their own. In reality this never happens. We know it, yet we still mow the lawn thinking they will.

This all sounds so neat, cozy, and cuddly in our lives. It all made sense to me when I wrote it down. It made even more sense when I researched it out. Then it made miraculous sense when I put it all in this book, but unless we apply it, it won't do a thing for us or help us heal or change our ways. The only way to rid our lives of the dandelions is to dig the roots out.

Unless I work on the puzzle and put it all together it will just be a pile of brokenness lying on the floor. It will be a mass of pieces, which by themselves won't help anybody, yet alone myself. This part of the equation is a reality. It will never change. It is what it is until I put forth my hand to correct and solve the situation!

When you open a jigsaw puzzle and dump out all the pieces on the floor or table, you have one great big mess. The picture on the front of the box looks so cool and wonderful, but to achieve your goal you have to pick up all the pieces and figure it all out.

You have to methodically put all the pieces in order so they fit. Figuring it all takes cunning, skill, and creativity. The hardest most difficult thing is not methodically putting it all together, it is formulating the method. It is coming up with an approach.

This was everything to me, and it is what I want to convey the most from all of this writing. My approach helped me discover the very things, which caused all my hurt. It was not just the things which caused it, but it was me. All of this led to me, to my hurt, to the violations in my life, which hurt my Core Value. It was my wounded soul, which was the issue. What an ultimate miracle for me, to discover the issues were those of my own heart!

So many hold onto the hurt and in turn inflict pain and abuse on others. Some hold on to it all their lives and are never free and always a victim. They use drugs, alcohol, sex, and other things to fill their lives and sadly they never acknowledge the puzzle or enigma is a scattered mess, let alone attempt to solve it.

Many quit just before the miracle happens

God bless them all, but they will die victims and never experience the satisfaction of becoming a survivor. They will never experience becoming a victor. They will never experience what they can learn and apply to their lives. We are all destined to be a blessing to others. In reality we are the very miracle others need; we just do not know it. Before we realize this, we quit, or are consumed with our own self pity over our situation.

In turn, they never will be able to share their satisfaction with others. Their victories will never touch another life because they have failed to experience life beyond being a victim. They never become the miracle they should have been.

Notes chapter 4

[1] Retrieved from http://www.jigsaw-puzzle.org   Retrieved January 22, 2011

[2] Kendall G., Parkes A. and Spoerer K. (2008) A   Survey of NP-Complete Puzzles, International   Computer Games Association Journal, 31(1), pp   13-34

[3] Compassion power.com

The backyard of my home in Seven Hills, Ohio

<u>Chapter Five</u>
Is it in color, or is it in black and white?

"Do to others whatever you would like them to do to you. This is the essence of all, which is taught in the law and the prophets." Jesus Christ, Mathew 7:12

I love this picture of my backyard. Even though it was taken in full color, it still looks black and white. This is what an abusive relationship is like. We keep trying to make our colorful relationship work, but it still looks and turns out black and white. Our situation is what it is. It's abusive, and if we don't deal with it, it will always be abusive.

Psychological abuse, which is also referred to as emotional abuse and mental abuse, is characterized by a person subjecting or exposing another to behavior, which is psychologically harmful. It also can lead others to engage in activity, which is against their better judgment.

You cannot see clearly because of the abuse. You tell people you are alright with everything, yet the picture is black and white to you and not color, but you think it is in color. The problem is what you are seeing as color, is black and white, but you think the black and white is the color. Others who are untrained believe you when you say, "it's in color." Yet, your responses tell them your vision is in black and white.

Such psychological abuse is often associated with situations of power imbalance. In abusive relationships, bullying, child abuse, and mistreatment in the work place is common place.

This I can associate with in my life from when I was a child. I was bullied by others, a lot. I still have memories of running home from school after having to slip out a back door to avoid the bully from beating me up. Yes, I was afraid, and for good reason; I did not want to get beat up, I did not want to experience pain!

On one occasion a bully kid chased me home from school. Along the way I had to hide in the bushes in front of someone's house. One time I remember holding my breath because he was so close but could not see me as I hid in the bushes. I remember being terrified beyond comprehension. I hated those days and all those kids who bullied me and terrorized my childhood.

I grew up resenting those kids and it was a great pleasure to me as I grew up when one at a time they were caught by police for having broken the law in one way or another. During this time of my life I did anything I had to, to avoid the pain. I think about those times now briefly.

No matter if I ran or not, the fear of the encounter terrified me. What is the most interesting fact is I remember being bullied, I remember being chased, but for the life of me to this day, I cannot remember what the bullies name was!

I carried those hurts most of my life. Some I discarded and others I carried well into my adult years. On one occasion in high school, I still remember it vividly; I finally confronted the fears of my childhood. I finally got tired of running and hiding.

I was in geometry class in 10th grade and was asked to go to the blackboard to solve a problem. Yes we used blackboards, and with real chalk! I was walking up the isle to the chalkboard and another kid returning from the chalkboard passed me and said something to me, what, I cannot remember. I only remember just ignoring him.

I was at the chalkboard with my back to the class when all of a sudden an eraser hit the chalkboard next to me. Poof, there was a cloud of chalk all around my head. I turned to see this kid standing there about 10 feet away just laughing at me and the whole class joining him to his delight. They were all laughing and pointing at me, I felt totally humiliated. My emotions then turned to rage and I remember feeling something, which I had never felt before in my life.

What actually happened next I still cannot remember? My next recollection was of the dean of students (who was the football coach) and 3 other male teachers pulling me off this kid on the floor.

The football coach and the others were not in the classroom; in fact their offices were down the hall and on the next floor. So it must have taken them some time to get there. When they pulled me off this kid he was a bloody mess, had a loose tooth, fat lip, and his shirt was ripped to shreds. It took four male adults in peak condition to pry me from this kid. My recollection now is I just totally snapped and just beat this kid to a pulp!

The nun teaching the class was screaming and yelling "O my God, O my God" and all the rest of the class was in shock. All the students were out of their seats, they were all standing up against the walls; all the girls were crying: desks, books, and coats were everywhere. It was quite a scene, total pandemonium!

All the years of running, hiding in bushes, being terrified, living in fear, and being bullied was pent up inside and all the pain, hurt, fear, humiliation, and torture just came out. This poor kid suffered for all the others who picked on me my whole life.

Glad to say the bullying against me really was curtailed after this event. All the abuse, both physical and psychological, and fear was dealt with on this day, but it was not totally over yet. As with every demon you exorcize in your life, they always come back just to check and see if they can fit in again. This happens only if you let them.

About a week later I was in the cafeteria of the school carrying my lunch tray. I was minding my own business. The reactions of the prior events of my classmates were pretty mixed. I was not the most popular kid, so some thought it was cool, some did not know what to think, and then there is the one, which stands out and has to check and see if it was legit.

This was the guy I crossed paths with when carrying my lunch tray in the cafeteria. I was walking and minding my own business, (really I was!). When I passed this kid and he said to me, "hey Skotko so you think you are tough" Now this kid wasn't a bully, in fact we kind of got along, not chummy, but we got along.

I just ignored him and kept walking. Then he says to me, "Don't ignore me." I thought he was kidding around because we never had an altercation before.

So he says to me again, "I said don't ignore me and he pushed me from behind and started laughing." I stumbled forward, and BAM, my tray hit the floor, my lunch went everywhere and into a girls lap, and the last thing I remember is turning and seeing him laughing and walking away from me.

Well guess what, the next thing I remember is the football coach pulling me off of him and the whole cafeteria shouting, "Fight, Fight, and Fight" I remember sitting in the coach's office all afternoon cooling down. Man I was really ticked this time. This kid had his shirt all torn up, and was sent home suspended for 3 days. This kid never said another word to me. In fact when he saw me after this, he would run and hide.

Only this time the football coach watched the whole thing happen and came to my defense. I got away unscathed from this fight. From that day forward, no one, and I mean no one in high school, ever picked on me again, or called me a name, or even messed with me in any sort of way!

On this day, I completely tore down the altar of fear from my childhood. This one event triggered my retaliation. All the other events over my life previous were building up to this point. The years of bullying and emotional and psychological abuse in my life as a child began to turn around.

I don't know if this was the correct way to deal with my fear, but it certainly helped me when I was young. Obviously as adults we could go around and beat people up, but it would probably land us in jail. Government has tried to put a rope on abuse. The efforts of law enforcement to curb domestic violence have had its positive points as well as the negative. The number one reported event, which causes law enforcement to suffer harm or death are domestic violence calls.

As of 1996, [1] there were no consensus views about the definition of emotional abuse from a government entity; as such since then, clinicians and researchers have offered sometimes divergent definitions of emotional abuse. However, Law enforcement personnel, Clinicians, and therapists use the Conflict Tactics Scale.

"The Conflict Tactics Scales, or CTS and CTS II (Straus, 1979, 1990s), [A] measures both the extent to, which partners in a dating, cohabiting, or marital relationship engage in psychological and physical attacks on each other and also their use of reasoning or negotiation to deal with conflicts.

Throughout my 25 year marriage, my ex-wife always gave me a hard time if I ever spoke to a member of the opposite sex. Nothing was ever happening or even conceived in an inappropriate way, it was just conversation; maybe at the library, supermarket, or even at church. This made living uneasy and difficult at times especially being involved in open public forums like church and social gatherings.

Plus the fact my natural personality is outgoing, friendly, and spontaneous made it extremely difficult. Often times we did not attend public functions or I attended them myself without her. I made huge concessions regarding how I had to "properly" conduct myself when I was in my ex-wife's presence.

This mentality on her part slowly progressed to total isolation, which in turn affected me. I was to discover later after we were separated how much I resented her for my having to make these concessions during our marriage.

For a period of about 5 years during our marriage I traveled extensively with my work. When I was at home during these 5 years, it was usually during the weekends. This absence on my part seemed to quench the fires of mistrust in my home. When we were together on the weekends there was peace. It was as if we weren't together for long enough periods of time to rekindle the psychological abuse, which forged the mistrust. What is odd about this is she never accused me of anything inappropriate during the week when I was away. She only accused me of inappropriate behavior during the times we were together.

Near the end of my marriage she would watch me as we just drove the car down the street. If there was a female walking, then the attention went toward me to see if I was, "checking her out?" When we were together at the store or other shopping place, she never let me converse with anyone of the opposite sex including cashiers. If I happened to be able to engage in conversion with anyone else, she would create an argument once we reached the car or got home.

Also prevalent on her part was the manipulation if I did not sever ties with my family. In 2003 I wrote a letter to my mother and sisters stating I was severing ties. I was led to believe by my ex-wife they had somehow perpetrated crimes against my children. This was direct counsel she received from her pseudo "Christian counselor," Marion Knox. She threatened to leave me and take the children if I did not do this.

During this particular time, my mind and emotions were racked with confusion and fear. I never gave it a thought that she was suffering from a mental breakdown, which I believe now was a result of her counseling sessions with Marion Knox. She threatened to leave me and take the kids and flee when I least expected it. This would have been because I would not have protected my children from the "real" perpetrators at this time, which were in her eyes, my mother and rest of my family.

It eventually led to her terminating relationships with her family as well. The episode, which dealt with her family, was she supposedly claimed to have caught her father sexually sodomizing our children. Yet she never called the police on them, as she did on me.

Over time this behavior led us to terminate all association with people because as she said, either she was uncomfortable with the man thinking he was making moves on her or she was uncomfortable with the woman thinking she was making moves on me.

This eventually led us to not have any kind of friendships with anyone. I was always puzzled in the fact I had a lot of personal acquaintances and she did not over the years of our marriage. She isolated herself. She wrapped all her time into the children, which was not bad. She was also so uncomfortable with any of my employees because everyone was threat of harm to the children or to her. This fear gripped her life to the point where she could not function normally.

Eventually, there was no one left in our lives to blame and ultimately because I failed to deal with the issues along the way, the blame had to shift to me. I was the only one left in her life to blame. It was this type of behavior on her part, which led me to "cutting ties" to my family because of a threat.

I realized my circumstances in my life did not happen all at once; it was years in the making. So also were the decisions by my ex-wife to take the actions she did; it was a process in the making for a long period during our marriage.

They have stated it was I who was the instigator and perpetrator. In reality, it was her with the coaching of her mad man counselor and therapist. I know now it will probably take years for anything to be healed and rectified concerning my relationship with my children.

This I believe also led to the tearing of my relationships with my children as they spent a lot of time with her. When the false accusation of abuse toward my children arose, the stories were strikingly similar to my ex-wife's stories of her childhood. These stories by my ex-wife came out after she began seeing the unlicensed counselor. Like I stated, ages, places, and types were all similar to what she claimed were her abuses as a child.

The U.S. Department of Justice defines emotionally abusive traits as including: causing fear by intimidation, threatening physical harm to self, partner, children, or partner's extended family or friends, destruction of pets and property, forcing isolation from family, friends, at school or work.[2]

Health Canada argues emotional abuse is motivated by urges for "power and control,"[3] and defines emotional abuse as including rejecting, degrading, terrorizing, isolating, corrupting,/exploiting, and "denying emotional responsiveness" as characteristic of emotional abuse. [B]

Societal conditioning

This takes us back to conditioning in society where certain things are unacceptable for men. Men are not to report any sort of behavior, which would be construed as abuse from the woman (domestic violence). This however leads to the mentioned "crimes" when law enforcement becomes involved (this is the 80%). (refer to footnotes.)

This leaves most statistics unbalanced and unreliable. This is why I probably did not even consider the idea of psychological abuse coming from my ex-wife or coming from her through her fake counselor.

Recent studies show reported emotional abuses in the workplace vary with these studies showing up to 36% of respondents indicating persistent and substantial emotional abuse from coworkers.

I believe we as a society have been conditioned over a long period. I have seen first-hand how men are conditioned and how this reflects in the way men treat women and the amount of nonsense, which is required of men by the courts and social workers investigations.

Religious conditioning

My involvement in fundamental religion has included protestant Pentecostal, Independent Full Gospel, and in my younger days Catholicism. I believe the fundamentalist views of religions, which have developed in male-dominated cultures, tend to reinforce emotional abuse.

Both Religious and secular critics contend all the major world religions historically taught the dominance of men over women. Most citing the Book of Genesis as an example of a text, which has been used to justify men abusing women: "in sorrow thou shall bring forth children: and thy desire shall be to thy husband, and he shall rule over you."

Fundamentalist religious prohibitions against divorce make it more difficult for religious women to leave an abusive marriage: A 1980s survey of Methodist clergy found 21% of them agreed no amount of abuse would justify a woman's leaving her husband.

Many other denominations including Southern Baptist and Assemblies of God place a requirement upon perspective individuals seeking ordination they have never been divorced or once they are divorced must terminate their ordination and can no longer carry credentials. In Catholicism, priests cannot marry and are required to maintain celibacy.

This behavior has a ripple down effect upon children who witness the hypocrisy of clergy and even the behavior of parents in the family setting. In society many older and some not so old children's stories contain gender stereotyping.

Music videos and computer games for children and teenagers have been criticized for continuing to portray men as aggressive and in control, while the females are there only for their sexual allure; women are portrayed as wanting to be chased and caught when they run away [14].

The same critics argue legal systems have in the past endorsed these traditions of male domination and it is only in recent years abusers have begun to be punished for their behavior. However, rebuttals note some laws in past centuries have specifically prohibited punitive wife-beating [15].

This all lends credence to the way most law enforcement agencies and court systems who give an enormous amount of credibility to the female complaints of sexual, emotional, and psychological abuse.

In most of the instances these agencies of the government place the sole blame on the male. In many cases the male is seen and treated as guilty until proven innocent. Many times even after exoneration the male carries the stereotype as still guilty and having just "beaten the system."

Personally, launching out to speak my mind concerning religious systems will probably not fare well with some of those who I have managed to maintain a certain amount of credibility with. I have discovered things, which I believe to be the truth. I am therefore compelled to make those discoveries known.

My focus is in finding and understanding the causes of abusive lifestyles. I began by examining my own life first. I have seen and witnessed these abuses within church walls, which has been acceptable for years if not centuries. This often leaves me befuddled as to why abusive behaviors creep into the church atmosphere where they claim to have the power to bring a deliverance from this sort of lifestyle.

I also feel personally the ecclesiastical church body as a whole has failed in addressing these issues. What is needed is a change to these preconceived ideas of the church leadership and the church body as a whole. I believe churches engage in this type of counseling without requirements of education and training because of the gross mistakes of government counterparts. This leads to lay-counselors such as Knox.

Once we learn and understand circumstances I believe we are responsible to react to them. If we ignore the truth once we learn it and this truth happens to be in contrary to the way we have functioned, it is our responsibility to change, no matter how painful the outcome.

It is our responsibility, whether in a church setting or society, to speak out against the conduct we now have learned to be an injustice. We become accountable and should we not respond, we should be held in the same light as those who created the problem.

Notes Chapter 5:

[1] Thompson AE, Kaplan CA. "Childhood emotional abuse." _British Journal of Psychiatry_, 1996 Feb; 168(2):143-8. PMID: 8837902

[2] US Department of Justice.

[3] www.phac-aspc.gc.ca/ncfv-cnivf/familyviolence/pdfs/emotion.pdf Emotional Abuse]". 1996. ISBN 0-662-24593-8

[4] Vachss, Andrew. 1994. "You Carry the Cure In Your Own Heart." _Parade_, 28 August 1994.

[5] Tomison, Adam M and Joe Tucci. 1997. Emotional Abuse: The Hidden Form of Maltreatment. Issues in Child Abuse Prevention Number 8, spring 1997.

[6] Bograd, M., Feminist perspectives on wife abuse: An introduction, in Bograd, M., and Yllo, K. eds., Feminist Perspectives on Wife Abuse, Sage Publishing, Beverly Hills, 1988; p 13.

[7] Dobash, R. E., and Dobash, R. P., Violence against wives: A case against the patriarchy, Free Press, New York, 1979., p.57

[8] Walker, L., Psychology and violence against women, American Psychologist, 44, 4, p. 695-702, 1989.

[9] Rennison, Callie Marie (February 2003)
(PDFNCJ 197838). *Intimate Partner Violence, 1993-2001.*
Bureau of Justice Statistics.

[10] Straus, M. A. (1999). The controversy over domestic violence by
women: A methodological, theoretical, and sociology of
science analysis. In X. P. Arrage & S. Oskamp (Eds.), Violence
in intimate relationships (pp. 17-44). Thousand Oaks, CA: Sage.

[11] Crime in England and Wales, Home Office, July 2002

[12] Straus, M. A., Hamby, S. L., Boney-McCoy, S., & Sugarman, D.
B. (1996). "The revised Conflict Tactics Scale (CTS-
2)." *Journal of Family Issues*, 17, pp. 283-317.

[13] Namie, G. (2000, October). *U.S. Hostile Workplace   Survey
2000*, Paper presented at the New England Conference on
Workplace Bullying, Suffol University Law School, Boston.

[14] Moore, Thomas Geoffrey; Marie-France Hirigoyen; Helen Marx
(2004). *Stalking the Soul: Emotional Abuse and the Erosion of
Identity*. New York: Turtle Point Press. pp. 196. ISBN 1885586-
99 X.

[15] "The Body of Liberties adopted in 1641 by the Massachusetts Bay
colonist's states, 'Every married woman shall be free from
bodily correction or stripes by her husband, unless it be in his

own defense from her assault."'

[www.mediaradar.org/docs/RADARreport-50-DV Myths.pdf]

[16] http://pubpages.unh.edu/~mas2/CTS15.pdf

[A] the most frequent application of the CTS has been to obtain data on physical assaults on a partner." [16]

The CTS and CTS II measures roughly 20 distinct acts of "psychological aggression" in three different categories; those categories are as follows:

1. Verbal aggression (e.g., "Your partner or someone in authority has said something to upset or annoy you");
2. Dominant behaviors (e.g., "I have tried to prevent my partner from seeing or speaking to their family. Childhood bullying falls into this category);
3. Jealous behaviors (e.g., "Your partner has accused you of maintaining other parallel relations or peers tear you down (foolish jesting) in order to diminish your self-worth, thereby positioning themselves in a superior hierarchy than you").

[B]   Andrew Vachss, an author, attorney and former sex crimes investigator, defines emotional abuse as "the systematic diminishment of another. It may be intentional or subconscious (or both), but it is always a course of conduct, not a single event."[4]

Subtler emotionally abusive tactics include insults, putdowns, arbitrary and unpredictable inconsistency, and gas-lighting (the denial previous abusive incidents occurred). Modern technology has led to new forms of abuse, by text messaging and online cyber-bullying.

Several studies have argued, unlike physical and sexual maltreatment, an isolated incident *does not* constitute emotional abuse. Tomison and Tucci write, "Emotional abuse is characterized by a climate or pattern of behavior(s) occurring over time. Thus, 'sustained' and 'repetitive' are the crucial components of any definition of emotional abuse."[5]

Feminist scholars [6] argue hundreds or thousands of years of male dominated societies have created negative attitudes towards women among many men, and wife abuse stems from "normal psychological and behavioral patterns of most men. Feminists seek to understand why men in general use physical force against their partners and what functions this serves for a society in a given historical context".

Similarly, Dobash and Dobash [7] claim "Men who assault their wives are actually living up to cultural prescriptions, which are cherished in Western society--aggressiveness, male dominance, and female subordination. They are using physical force as a means to enforce dominance", while Walker [8] claims men exhibit a "socialized andro-centric need for power".

While some women are aggressive and dominating to male partners the majority of abuse in heterosexual partnerships, at about 80% in the USA, is by men.

[9] (Note: critics [10] stress this Department of Justice study examines *crime* figures, and does not specifically address *domestic abuse* figures. While the categories of crime and domestic abuse may cross-over, most instances of domestic abuse are *not* regarded as crimes or reported to police—critics thus argue it's inaccurate to regard the DOJ study as a comprehensive statement on domestic abuse because

compelling evidence shows men and women tend to commit emotional and physical abuse in roughly equal rates.)

A 2002 study reports ten percent of violence in the UK, overall, is by females against males [11]. However, more recent data specifically regarding domestic abuse (including emotional abuse) report 3 in 10 women, and 2 in 10 men, have experienced domestic abuse [12].

Namie found males and females commit "emotionally abusive behaviors" in the workplace at roughly similar rates. In a web-based survey, Namie also found women were more likely to engage in workplace bullying, such as name-calling, and the average length of abuse was 16.5 months [13].

Chapter Six
The Capable Realm of God

"The challenge in life is to live beyond what you think is possible into the realm of what God knows you are capable of." – Mark Brown

In my first book, "A Heart Held Ransomed" My attempt was to express my story. The initial results and feedback of the book have been positive. I am eternally thankful to those who have rallied behind me and have supported me throughout this time. On September 18, 2008, my life as I knew it ended. This is what I wanted to convey to you in the previous chapters, my past.

In September of 2008, I suddenly found myself on a battlefield, fighting a war, I did not choose, and wanted nothing to do with! I fully realize now, four years later I am a man facing an adversary bent on destroying many and so I fight my battle forward.

As I write these words, I am in the midst of waiting on information for the direction my litigation is going to follow. A judge has already allowed the lawsuit to proceed forward, farther than anyone expected. We have just completed depositions. With a court reporter present; she transcribed what my attorney and the opposition's attorney asked during two days of unending questions of both parties. Then this case will be argued back and forth in summary judgment. Then it will either settle or go to trial. At this point a jury will decide whether enough evidence has been presented or if more evidence will need to be presented regarding my lawsuit.

The night the depositions ended I was driving to the place I was staying near Corvallis, Oregon. As I drove an overwhelming feeling came over me. It was an overpowering feeling. It was as if my enemy was staring me in the face attempting to devastate me. It was trying to crush me. Suddenly I felt so alone and helpless.

"What do I do now?" I said out loud.

As I continued to drive I began to pray and cry out to God,

 "Lord I don't know what to do now. I feel so overwhelmed, so insignificant. I need you God!"

I did not know what to do. I had been fighting this battle for over three years. I fought through all the false allegations and had won. Now, again, fear tried to creep into my heart. Fear was attempting to crush me yet again. I felt as if I had been fighting this battle uphill for 3 years. Now as I reached the apex of this hill a vast landscape laid in front of me to now conquer. I was completely exhausted. My energy was spent! I just drove the car and prayed.

Being in Oregon again brought me mixed emotions and memories. The car seemed to melt into the rain drenched road as my mind raced back and forth. Time seemed to stand still and then it quickly sped up. I reached the residence where I was staying and went to dinner with my friend Gale. I talked to him about how tired and exhausted I was.

When I returned home from dinner I went to sleep early. On this night I had a dream. This dream would set me free. I believe with all my heart, God gave me this dream in answer to my prayers. He spoke to me through this dream, it was profound!

In the dream I was in a large steel building, a garage with tall ceilings. I stood up and stepped back and I saw before me what looked to be the beginnings of an automobile. The frame was there, and it had 4 wheels. I began to push it and it rolled along pretty easily. I pushed it to the other end of the room. There was standing, my Attorney Dan. I then woke up and immediately I felt as if God told me,

"Steve your job is finished for now; there is nothing more you can do at this point. Now it is Dan's turn. Relax and get some rest and we will take care of the rest."

I have never felt more at ease. God used the word "we." It was as if a huge weight I had been carrying was gone. There I was lying in my bed, in the dark at 2:00 in the morning I knew that I knew, the situation was In God's hands and He was going to move through my attorney. God was going to partner now with my attorney.

The next day I asked Gale,

"Was I even coherent last night at dinner?"

"Barely, he replied."

The dream was so real and alive, when I awoke in the middle of the night, I was taken back: I was almost out of breath. The dream was acute. This dream was food for me, a hungry traveler. The dream was for me. It filled me back up.

As I have constantly stated, I am not doing this for monetary gain. In fact the opposite is true. I tried early on to forget everything and somehow go on. But always, someone else approached me to encourage me on. My story is one vehicle by which I believe steps are being taken to end the unorthodox therapy wielded by self proclaimed therapists, who teach about repressed memories. This particular part of the journey was over; now the next valley and battle terrain stood ahead of us.

Sadly, these unorthodox measures are being carried out mostly by men and women hiding behind the cloak of clergy, or untrained lay ministers, church members, and self-proclaimed false prophets with the approval of her or his leadership.

On Sunday July 10th, 2011 the Albany, Oregon, Democrat Herald ran a story entitled "Repressed Memory Therapy continues in the mid-valley." Opponents of the article are those who perform this type of "inner healing" in many churches. This was the papers 8th article concerning my story.

These pseudo-therapists claim they are qualified to conduct this therapy. They are neither licensed nor formally trained. They carry no degrees. It is precisely these types of counselors who carry on this sort of counseling or therapy, without any guidelines, laws, or ethical standards whatsoever. In doing so they cannot be held responsible for any of their methods; this is what I want to see stopped [2].

I love the church. I love going to church. I enjoy everything churches do. I enjoy the bible studies, meeting people, reaching out to people. I enjoy gatherings of men's groups, bible studies, and all other ministries. But there is a point I believe the church in some areas has overstepped itself. Unlicensed therapy is one of these areas. Therapy in and of itself is not bad, **but to lead an individual down a prescribed path of the counselors choosing is immensely wrong.**

Along my journey, others have stepped forward to help and encourage me when I needed it most. I remember after I first began working with my friend Teila Tankersley on "A Heart Held Ransomed; she published a few stories on the net. One of the other affected families saw her article and found my email address and asked me if he could forward her articles to the local newspaper in Albany, Oregon. I said, absolutely go ahead. He did, and that decision wound up spinning into 7 articles in the paper over a period of 6 months. It included a 5 day series over Memorial Day weekend 2011. The Eighth article I just listed above. Those stories spurred many families to contact the paper with similar stories as mine.

Things like this began to happen. I just kind of went along for the ride. When my ordeal first began in 2008, it was tough sledding for about 9 months. Then when my Department of Human Services hearing was ended I began to pray and told God,

"Lord, you know I don't want to sue anyone for money, but somehow God, this stuff has got to stop. If you want me to carry this on, then you will have to speak to me, because this is racking me Lord. I won't go down this road by myself, but somehow I sense it is not over, please Lord help me or give me peace and closure on all of this."

The next day after praying this prayer in the summer of 2009 and I mean it was the next day, my attorney called me. He told me,

"Steve, we need to stop this guy. If you want, I will represent you on a contingency basis. I think we need to do all we can to stop him."

I took this as an answer to my prayer. Case closed!

Oh, by the way, my attorney **never** takes things on a contingency basis, so this in itself is a miracle! Then the same day when I was speaking to my friend Gale he said to me,

"Steve I believe you are the one chosen to fight this battle."
Case closed again!

I have nothing against good therapy and counseling, and I
believe if you need it, you should seek it out. Everyone involved in a
church should have a good relationship with your pastor or priest. You
should be confident you can approach him or her at any time and seek
guidance.

I believe, all individuals who present themselves as counselors
or therapists in any form including leadership, should carry merited
credentials or formal education. At least he or she should counsel within
their given credentials. They should not **lead** people into believing
something happened to them.

For over 25 years I was a self employed general contractor. I
have come to discover there were more laws, regulations, and state
licensing requirements of me, than there are on church based
counselors. Not only was my profession required to have licensing, but
also, landscapers, plumbers, electricians, and a host of other
construction trades. How much more should those who claim the ability
to cure a person's mind and soul, be held accountable and require
licensing?

Over the last year and a half, the newspaper in Albany, Oregon,
has printed a dozen stories concerning all of the circumstance of my
life. 97% has been positive. I believe these individuals wearing their
cloak of clergy and untrained church counselor's, need to be held
accountable and fall under some sort of rules, guidelines, or code of
ethics, in which they administer their therapy. Everyone seems to
support our views except for unlicensed church counselors. It is these

unlicensed people who are against it and support the theory of repressed memories.

In my case it is too late, the damage has been done. The scars left upon my family are forever because of these unorthodox methods of therapy. Marion Knox ravaged my life and the lives of my children and immediate family. I want Knox and others to stop. I want other potential victims to be informed, so the same thing will not happen to them. I do not ever want to hear of another family being destroyed by this unorthodox therapy.

People ask me often, "How do you do it. How are you hanging in there the way you are. You are in school, and you have written a book. How do you do it?"

In my eyes I am not hanging in there with anything. This is my calling, this is my job. It is not over and probably never will be. It will always be a part of my life. In this way it is OK, because I am witnessing others becoming aware and being set free as a result of my trials. This is my challenge in life. This is the capable realm of God for my life. God is leading me and sustaining me through this experience. I desire to be the miracle for others experiencing the same thing.

I never want anyone to ever be hurt again by the same sort of screwball, unorthodox, church-based unlicensed counseling. Every day presents itself with a whole new set of challenges and circumstances to overcome. I just take it one day at a time, baby steps!

I ask people this, "If you saw a burning house and heard a baby crying inside, would you risk your life and attempt to save the helpless child?" I know I would! This is what I am attempting to do. I want to save the lives and homes of families who do not even know the enemy is stalking them; ready to move in for the kill.

I am reminded in history of Sgt. Alvin C. York, one of my favorite persons from history. Gary Cooper portrayed Sgt. York in a Hollywood movie in the 1940's. As depicted in the movie Alvin York was a simple farmer living in the mountains of Tennessee, when he was drafted into the United States Army in World War I. This is my favorite movie.

History teaches us Alvin York was a rowdy young man liking to dance and drink and just plain raise hell when he got the chance. On January 1, 1915 before he was drafted, Alvin had a dramatic conversion to Christianity, where he was literally knocked of his horse by a bolt of lightning.

As a result of his conversion, he originally protested his draft status by registering as a conscientious objector, based on his Christianity. He was turned down at the local level, county level, state and federal levels.

Alvin's congregation was the Church of Christ in Christian Union, a Protestant denomination. This denomination shunned secular politics and disputes between other Christian denominations. This denomination had no specific doctrine of pacificism but had been formed in reaction to the Methodists' support for the Civil War and now opposed all forms of violence. [1]

In a lecture later in life, Alvin reported his reaction to the outbreak of World War I:

"I was worried clean through. I didn't want to go and kill. I believed in my bible."

On June 5, 1917, at the age of 29, Alvin York registered for the draft as all men between 21 and 31 years of age did in those days. When he registered for the draft, he answered the question "Do you claim exemption from draft (specify grounds)?" by writing "Yes. Don't Want To Fight." When his initial claim for conscientious objector status was denied, he appealed. [1]

During World War I, conscientious objector status did not exempt one from military duty. Such individuals could still be drafted and were given non-combative assignments, which did not conflict with their anti-war principles. In November 1917, while York's application was considered, he was drafted and began his army service. [1]

From the day he registered for the draft until he returned from the war on May 29, 1919, York kept a diary of his activities. In his diary, York wrote a refusal to sign documents provided by his pastor seeking a discharge from the Army on religious grounds and refused to sign similar documents provided by his mother asserting a claim of exemption as the sole support of his mother and siblings. He also disclaimed ever having been a conscientious objector. [1]

He reluctantly left for the United States Army to fight in a war he did not feel called to and first served at Camp Gordon, Georgia before being deployed to France. While the Army kept their eyes on York, he had one thing, which was extremely beneficial to the Army; he could shoot a rifle. Actually he was an expert marksman and was quickly promoted to the rank of corporal before his deployment to France.

"Alvin Cullum York was born December 13, 1887, died September 2, 1964. He became one of the most decorated American soldiers in World War I. He received the Congressional Medal of Honor for leading an attack on a German machine gun nest, taking 32 machine guns, killing 28 German soldiers and capturing 132 others."

This action occurred during the U.S. led portion of the Meuse-Argonne Offensive in France, which was part of a broader Allied offensive masterminded by Marshal Ferdinand Foch, to breach the Hindenburg line and make the opposing German forces to surrender. [1]

Before his return he was asked why he did what he did, because the Army knew of his conscientious objector status based on religious freedoms and his convictions not to kill anyone. His reply resounds with character, and it is the same reason why I am fighting my ordeal the way I am. Sergeant Alvin York stated the following,

"The Germans got us, and they got us right smart. They just stopped us dead in our tracks. Their machine guns were up there on the heights overlooking us and well hidden, and we couldn't tell for certain where the terrible heavy fire was coming from."

"I'm telling you they were shooting straight. Our boys just went down like the long grass before the mowing machine at home. Our attack just faded out... And there we were, lying down, about halfway across the valley and those German machine guns and big shells getting us hard."

"I was pinned up against this hill. And those machine guns were spitting fire and cutting down the undergrowth all around me something awful. And the Germans were yelling orders. You never heard such a racket in all of your life."

"I didn't have time to dodge behind a tree or dive into the brush... As soon as the machine guns opened fire on me, I began to exchange shots with them."

"There were over thirty of them in continuous action, and all I could do was touching the Germans off just as fast as I could. I was sharp shooting... All the time I kept yelling at them to come down. I didn't want to kill any more than I had to. They kept shooting at me, so I just kept picking them off, one by one, front to back, like a flock of wild turkey!"

"It was they or I. And I was giving them the best I had. Now I am against killing now as I always have been. But, I saw my men, my friends dropping like flies all around me. Those machine guns were killing dozens if not hundreds of my men and my friends. I knew I had to stop them machine guns before they killed anymore."

The general questioning York then looked at York and said, "You mean to tell me you did what you did to save lives and not take lives?"

To which York replied, "Yes sir, that is what I am saying"

The general replied, "This is the most remarkable thing I think I have ever heard." The general then asked York's commanding officer where the rest of York's unit was during this time.

The commanding officer replied, "The men have stated they were under heavy fire and could not move without fear of death."

It is recorded in history the following,

"During the assault, six German soldiers in a trench near York charged him with fixed bayonets. York had fired all the rounds in his

M1917 Enfield rifle, but drew his colt .45 caliber pistols and shot all six soldiers with six bullets dead before they could reach him. [1]

German First Lieutenant Paul Jürgen Vollmer, commander of the First Battalion, 120th Landwehr Infantry, emptied his pistol trying to kill York while he was contending with the machine guns. Failing to injure York, and seeing his mounting losses, he offered in English to surrender the unit to York, who accepted. [1]

By the end of the engagement, York and the seven men, who were left marched 132 German prisoners back to the American lines. His actions silenced the German machine guns and were responsible for enabling the 328th Infantry to renew its attack to capture the Decauville Railroad. [1]"

Sgt. Alvin York was named the hero of the Argonne. The Argonne was a pivotal battle of the American forces in turning back the German army in World War I. York was paraded through New York City upon his return, given the key of the city, and Wall Street closed early on this day to celebrate York's return.

It was estimated Sgt. Alvin York received in the neighborhood of $250,000.00 in promotions for his heroics. Those propositions were presented to him by Congressman Cordell Hull who represented where York lived. Cordell Hull would later become secretary of state under Franklin Roosevelt.

Sgt. York turned down the money because as he stated,

"There are a lot of boys who went there, who aren't coming home. I do not think those kind of things are worth buying and selling.

So would you please tell them I am refusing those offers and I am going home?"

Later York relented a bit and agreed to the Hollywood film "Sergeant York" to fund a bible school. The film won a best actor academy Oscar award for Gary Cooper, and was nominated for 11 others.

Sergeant York, a man I extremely admire from history was a man of character and principle. If only I could portray the same in a small amount. I know it would make a difference. He did what he needed to do, without regard for his own life or safety. He was not worried about himself, but for the others who were being killed.

Within each and every one of us there exists the power and ability to overcome any obstacle, any abuse, and any injustice, which might be placed in our paths! I believe drugs and alcohol can be, and are most often emotional inhibitors to those who are suffering from abuse. They cause the one abused, to lose contact with their hurt. They disable those victims from engaging in the natural processes and decisions needed to bring healing. Anger is an emotional inhibitor for those performing the abuse. Anger is a result of abuse. It is a vicious cycle, which repeats itself over and over.

In my life, I have found tremendous strength and healing in reading and studying history, both through the Holy Bible and secular historical documents. I believe God gave me this deep interest of history as part of my personality. I receive tremendous healing through my reading and study through history.

I want to use the previous stories and history in the attempt to convey to you the reader, how these studies over my lifetime have helped me heal and go forward one day at a time. This is my capable realm of God!

Every individual seeking help and freedom from their pain and hurt must locate his or her gifting to achieve their healing. Using drugs and alcohol or being prescribed them I believe, hinders us in acknowledging our pain from abuse and eternal weakness. It places our focus and mindset to the fact we have become addicted to the drugs and alcohol we thought would help us. Addiction robs each and every one of those individuals from ever achieving their true calling in life and the expression of it to others. It keeps those individuals from his or her capable realm of God.

I have already, and want to share with you some of my favorite stories about people and how they overcame obstacles, influenced, and manipulated others, both positively and negatively. These stories have helped shape me and my outlook on life.

Jesus spoke from the cross these words,

"Father, forgive them, for they know not what they do."

I realized more than I ever did when I began this great journey; forgiveness is an act of my will, and not my emotions. If I waited until I felt like forgiving, I would live with bitterness in my heart. I knew bitterness would consume me, it would eventually destroy me.

Forgiveness is not for the person perpetrating the hurt towards you. The act of forgiveness heals you! Forgiveness sets you, the victim free. When you forgive you're not submitting to their abuse, brutality, or condoning their injustice toward you. You are not whitewashing the words or deeds of your offender.

You are forgiving to bring cleansing to you!

Forgive your enemies; it's the only way to liberate your mind and emotions from the toxic poison of the painful memory, abuse, or abusive situation.

Mathew 6:12-15 says,

"12 forgive us our sins as we have forgiven those who sin against us. 13 And don't let us yield to temptation, but rescue us from the evil one. 14 "If you forgive those who sin against you, your heavenly Father will forgive you; 15 but if you refuse to forgive others, your Father will not forgive your sins.

It doesn't matter if you feel you did not deserve how the other person treated you. Our heavenly Father knows exactly what it will take for us to be free.

The greatest story I can every convey is how Jesus Christ came and died for our sins. Nothing greater can ever be told by any person to another how this greatest sacrifice has changed my life forever. In the midst of the abuse Jesus received for things He did not do, He forgave them. If you do not know Jesus as your personal Lord and Savior, I invite you to just stop and pray and ask Him to be your Lord.

On May 27th 1980 at 5:27 PM in the barracks of Petersen AFB in Colorado Springs, Colorado, I prayed and received Jesus into my heart as my Lord and Savior. This single act was the best decision I have ever made in my life. My life was forever changed.

"There is no greater love than this; than a man lay down his life for a friend."

This is the Capable Realm of God!

Notes Chapter Six:

[1] Sergeant York Patriotic Foundation: Sgt Alvin C. York's Diary
October 8, 1918 accessed December 2011, and historic notes
and documents found in the Sergeant York Patriotic Foundation.

[2] This article can be found on the world-wide-web @
http://democratherald.com/repressed-memory-counseling-
continues-in-mid-valley/article_6849b3b2-aac9-11e0-9dc1-
001cc4c002e0.html

Chapter Seven
The Confrontation Begins

Habakkuk 1:4 states' *"The law has become paralyzed, and there is no justice in the courts. The wicked far outnumber the righteous; as a result, justice has become perverted."* (New Living Translation)

Most people view the Bible as a spiritual religious book. While this is true, the Bible is also a valuable book in the history of mankind and his or her relationship with God and each other.

God abhors injustice especially against people who acknowledge Him as Supreme God. Like I stated earlier, "Nothing just happens," God fully realizes what is happening and is letting it happen for a purpose.

Jesus Christ himself cried out against the religious leaders of His day. In today's world the equivalent would be Pastors, Priests, televangelists, theologians and political leaders who have attached the word Reverend to the front of their names.

Remember the Holy Bible was written for the Religious and not the sinner.

When Jesus spoke his words in Mathew chapter 23, he was speaking to church (religious) people including the leadership of them. Jesus cried out against the leaders because they built their religious empires (ministries) on the backs of the common people and those who had been abused by the political and religious system, which was in place.

Matthew chapter 23 is right on board for Jesus to proclaim the rewards of further abusing the common person, and those seeking a true and undefiled relationship with God. In this scripture Jesus proclaims how God views those who abuse their authority and suppress criticism; those who view themselves as perfect, and practice unbalanced teaching beliefs.

Matthew 23

Jesus Criticizes the Religious Leaders.

(Taken from the New Living Translation)

[1] Then Jesus said to the crowds and to his disciples, [2] "The teachers of religious law and the Pharisees are the official interpreters of the law of Moses. [3] So practice and obey whatever they tell you, but don't follow their example; because they don't practice what they teach. [4] They crush people with unbearable religious demands and never lift a finger to ease the burden.

[5] "Everything they do is for show. On their arms they wear extra wide prayer boxes with Scripture verses inside, and they wear robes with extra long tassels. [6] They love to sit at the head table at banquets and in the seats of honor in the synagogues. [7] They love to receive respectful greetings as they walk in the marketplaces, and to be called 'Rabbi.'

[8] "Don't let anyone call you 'Rabbi,' for you have only one teacher, and all of you are equal as brothers and sisters [9] Don't address anyone here on earth as 'Father,' for only God in heaven is your spiritual Father. [10] And don't let anyone call you 'Teacher,' for you have only

one teacher, the Messiah. [11] The greatest among you must be a servant. [12] But those who exalt themselves will be humbled, and those who humble themselves will be exalted.

[13] "What sorrow awaits you teachers of religious law and you Pharisees? Hypocrites! For you shut the door of the Kingdom of Heaven in people's faces. You won't go in yourselves, and you don't let others enter either.

[15] "What sorrow awaits you teachers of religious law and you Pharisees? Hypocrites! For you cross land and sea to make one convert, and then you turn this person into twice the child of hell you yourselves are!

[16] "Blind guides! What sorrow awaits you! For you say it means nothing to swear 'by God's Temple,' but it is binding to swear 'by the gold in the Temple.' [17] Blind fools! Which is more important—the gold or the Temple, which makes the gold sacred? [18] And you say to swear 'by the altar' is not binding, but to swear 'by the gifts on the altar' is binding. [19] How blind; for which is more important—the gift on the altar or the altar, which makes the gift sacred?

[20] When you swear 'by the altar,' you are swearing by it and by everything on it. [21] And when you swear 'by the Temple,' you are swearing by it and by God, who lives in it. [22] And when you swear 'by heaven,' you are swearing by the throne of God and by God, who sits on the throne.

[23] "What sorrow awaits you teachers of religious law and you Pharisees? Hypocrites! You are careful to tithe even the tiniest income

from your herb gardens, but you ignore the more important aspects of the law, which are justice, mercy, and faith. You should tithe, yes, but do not neglect the more important things. [24] *Blind guides! You strain your water so you won't accidentally swallow a gnat, but you swallow a camel!*

[25] *"What sorrow awaits you teachers of religious law and you Pharisees? Hypocrites! For you are so careful to clean the outside of the cup and the dish, but inside you are filthy—full of greed and self-indulgence!* [26] *You blind Pharisee! First wash the inside of the cup and the dish; then the outside will become clean, too.*

[27] *"What sorrow awaits you teachers of religious law and you Pharisees? Hypocrites! For you are like whitewashed tombs—beautiful on the outside but filled on the inside with dead people's bones and all sorts of impurity.* [28] *Outwardly you look like righteous people, but inwardly your hearts are filled with hypocrisy and lawlessness.*

[29] *"What sorrow awaits you teachers of religious law and you Pharisees? Hypocrites! For you build tombs for the prophets your ancestors killed, and you decorate the monuments of the godly people your ancestors destroyed.* [30] *Then you say, 'If we had lived in the days of our ancestors, we would never have joined them in killing the prophets.'*

[31] *"But in saying this, you testify against yourselves that you are indeed the descendants of those who murdered the prophets.* [32] *Go ahead and finish what your ancestors started.* [33] *Snakes! Sons of vipers! How will you escape the judgment of hell?*

34 "Therefore, I am sending you prophets and wise men and teachers of religious law. But you will kill some by crucifixion, and you will flog others with whips in your synagogues, chasing them from city to city.

35 As a result, you will be held responsible for the murder of all godly people of all time—from the murder of righteous Abel to the murder of Zechariah son of Brachia, whom you killed in the Temple between the sanctuary and the altar.

36 I tell you the truth; this judgment will fall on this very generation. [1]

Jesus said it plainly and to the point so the religious leaders would understand the severity of their attitudes, teachings, and lifestyles. While spiritual abuse may not take place in all church denominations, it is fairly prevalent in most of them. God's intention is for mankind to fall in love with him. Religion and religious systems do not cause us to fall in love with God. In fact they drive us further from the loving arms of God.

You cannot give away what you do not possess or have received yourself from God.

I want to state right now I am by no means against or pessimistic with regards to religion. In fact I enjoy attending a good healthy church and being with people who share in my beliefs. Probably the most criticism I bring is on me! How do I treat people? It is all about a relationship with Jesus Christ.

This is why Jesus was so ticked off at the religious leaders of his day. They were giving the people exactly what they had, and it was not from God. The religious leaders were hypocritical toward God; therefore, this is what they taught the common person. They were a highly organized system of dysfunction.

In my life I am a huge proponent of organization. There is a way, a system, I believe God created for the course of human history to unveil. I believe in God and I believe He is perfect. God cannot be bought, sold, or bartered with. Therefore, His established system is perfect, without blemish. Like the old saying, "God don't make any junk."

In God's system the Bible is our Anchor

I also believe each and everyone born can have a personal, intimate relationship with our God, in essence, our Creator, or in better terms; your God and your creator. God's perfect system for our lives only can be interrupted by one thing. This thing is sin. Sin is what separates us from God. The Word of God (the bible), gives us a reference point to keep us in check and help us avoid sin.

In using the word interrupted I mean sin takes us off course from God's perfect system. Sin sets us up in our own system, which at the time seems logical and makes perfect sense to us, but it is not God's system. In our system, we pull in the anchor and begin to drift. Sin causes us to drift aimlessly. We pull up our spiritual anchor because at that particular moment, our system appears to be better than God's. God never interrupts The System. We interrupt Gods system. In our man made system, there is no defined place to set anchor. The anchor in our system is what we choose when we choose it.

From a personal standpoint, I try to keep my life as organized as I can. Over the years this has saved my bacon and then again on the other hand, it has been my undoing. I remember my years in the United States Air Force and how we all needed to be organized. If you have never had the opportunity to spend time in the Military, you might not fully

Even in basic training, the drawer we kept our clothes in was exactly eighteen inches wide. This meant our underwear and undershirts had to be folded exactly in 6 in squares and placed next to each other. Then our handkerchiefs were in 3 inch squares and then a row of sox at 3 inches.

There was no room for overlap and there was no room for space. It had to be perfect. If it was not perfect the drill instructor would pull the drawer out and dump the contents on the floor, and we had to do it over again.

In basic training we were in squads of 50 men. We also had a sister squad, which was going through basic training at the same time we were. We competed against them in all facets of basic training. On one occasion while we were all in the day room adjacent to our living quarters, our drill instructor permitted our sister squad to come in and tear up our living quarters while we were made to sit and listen.

They had a grand time pulling our clothing drawers out and dumping them on the floor and kicking everything around. They tore our beds up, mixed up our clothes scuffed up the floors, urinated all over the bathroom, and dirtied our toilets. They completely trashed the place. Then we had to put it all back.

As we were beginning to start, our drill instructor told us we could not retaliate in any way. He also told us,

"You can wander around here like a bunch of sniveling babies or you could help each other by treating everyone else's stuff like our own."

This meant just start picking up clothes and putting them back in order. This is what we did. Some were better with undershirts, some were better with socks; some could make a bed better. so everyone just did what they were best at, and the job got done very quickly.

This was all meant so we would pay attention to detail and help our fellow man and work as a team. It also exercised our minds to develop into mentally strong individuals. All this was training if we were ever to find our way to a battle conflict setting. If all of us would be left to our own individual mental fortitude, we would all abandon our fellow troops in moments of extreme mental anguish should our lives be on the line.

One of the first jobs I had at my first duty station was files clerk. The Air Force sent me to special training and classes to learn the specifics of the Air Force filing system upon arriving at my first permanent duty station, NORAD in Colorado Springs.

Today a lot of filing and the system of filing has changed with the vast use of computers. In the time I learned the Air Force filing system there were no computers and there was no form of electronic filing systems in use. I was in charge of the files. If anyone pulled out a file, they were not permitted to put it back. This was my job and my job only. The others put them in a basket, I then replaced them.

My commanding officer back in 1980 told me pretty much in one sentence the importance of a proper filing system. "It does you no good to have everything documented if you can't find it when you need it." I have tried to carry this philosophy through my day-to-day life since then.

From a Christian standpoint it speaks volumes to me. We as believers should adhere to these words, however, God does not! God is perfect, God knows all, sees all, and the word says, "God rewards those who diligently seek Him." God does not have to keep things organized according to our standards because God is Organization. His Being is organization. He is God. He says it and it's over. You can't stop and tell God He is wrong because you have been hurt, or someone messed up the clothing of your life, because He is God.

Another term, which is loosely used is, "God is able." People like to use it when they themselves have failed. They think and have been taught that somehow God will respond in the midst of our failure. This is absolutely wrong. God never responds to any success or failure, which mankind brings upon them.

God responds only to faith!

Faith is, in the easiest way to describe, lining up yourself, your decisions, and your life with God. It is finally when you, the individual decide you are going to fold the issues of your life into 6 inch squares to fit into the draw, which God has provided you, and not the way you think it should be done. It is when you set anchor where God tells you, no matter what the circumstances or surroundings are!

God is not "able." God is!

When you start to realize this and line yourself up with it, then you will notice how easy things become.

A lot of people have a lot of problems with what I am saying. Over time I have discovered most of my problems are not because of God letting things happen. They are because of my sin and my lack of God's plan and organization, which has brought about my problems. Your problems always become apparent after you pull up your anchor from where God wants it and you put it where you want!

The beauty of God

Because of my shortcomings, rebellions, and sin, God permitted things to transpire. This is the beauty of God, He permits us to experience the ramifications of our poor decisions, so we will learn. In reality, it is not even God permitting them to happen. They happen as a part of the plan God put in place. This is a place where good parents error. They want to step in and save their children from the pain of their decisions. If you at this point can step back, you will realize these same circumstances are what shaped you as an individual.

In the Garden of Eden, God told Adam and Eve in Genesis 3:2-3 the following

[2] *"Of course we may eat fruit from the trees in the garden," the woman replied.* [3] *"It's only the fruit from the tree in the middle of the garden that we are not allowed to eat. God said, 'You must not eat it or even touch it; if you do, you will die.'"*

This was God's plan, every decision Adam and Eve made was according to this plan. This is the beauty of God. Any violation of God's instructions had irreversible consequences. It all came down to disobedience to God. This is sin!

God never responds to anything we do in the flesh no matter how sincere we are in doing them! God only responds to faith.

We all do not like the word sin. It has such negative connotations. The very sound of the word "sin" makes one think of something black, like being prodded by a sharp instrument. This is exactly what sin is.

When we think of sin we tend to think of some huge, big, hairy act against humanity. Like some serial killer or child abuser. Yet, basically sin is when we know to do something and do not do it. Sin is the small things we don't do. Sin is not returning being given to much change from the cashier. Sin is not answering our children with the truth when they ask you about uncomfortable things like sex.

I grew up in a Catholic home. I attended Catholic schools for a major part of my young life. In all these years I never read scripture, I never read the Word of God. I was never encouraged to read the Bible by anyone. Priests, nuns, teachers, parents, no one ever advised me to read the Bible.

During my young adult life, I believed in God. I believed in God's whole plan of Salvation. I believed in angels, demons, and the plethora of religious people, events, and things found in the bible. But I never read the Bible itself! I never learned about sin from God's standpoint. What a pleasant shock it was when I began reading the Bible. It was so interesting to me. The stories tell of mankind and his relationship with his God; the great victories and the great ramifications and consequences when man rebelled against God.

When you approach the Bible from a worldly intellectual mindset, the Bible can read to be dry, tasteless, and dull. However when you approach the Bible from an intimate, heartfelt love affair with your

God, the Bible is food; the Word of God is sustenance for the dry, longing need to be in

I believe with my whole heart the Bible is the only book you will ever read, which can read your thoughts. This is the only book you will ever read, which knows your heart. This is why when you read God's Word it can bring you discomfort. This is why when you read the Bible it can make you uneasy because it is alive. The discomfort and uneasiness is not how far out there or weird the Bible is; it is how weird and how far we have wandered from God!

The Bible is the essence of God through Holy Spirit penetrating you. God uses the Word in every occasion to bring you to the conformity of Jesus Christ (God with us). This is because of our sin nature. We naturally gravitate toward the things, which can lead us astray from our relationship with God.

It is a heart condition. It is an important part in being close with God; a part of lining up with His plan and organization for our lives. When we are close to God we will respond quickly when we feel He is compelling us. But life is like fishing in a boat. You are sitting there fishing. No cares, no wind, you are just enjoying yourself. All of a sudden you look up and you have drifted really far from where you started and you have to paddle back to stay on course, lest you drift into the rocks near the shore, crash, and drown.

It becomes difficult to respond to God, not because He asks a hard thing, it is because we have naturally drifted away from Him. It is so easy when helping and leading people to cross the line a bit and begin to control. This is what Jesus blasted in Mathew 23. God Himself does not seek to control people. Part of His organizational plan is to permit us to possess a free will to choose. Going back again in the Bible to the book of Genesis, we read about Adam and Eve.

We have all heard the stories of Adam and Eve, how Eve was tempted and ate the fruit, then turned and gave it to Adam. This is what caused us our sin nature.

It was through the act of "self will and choice," God chose to put everything we know into motion. Throughout the centuries every event was directly the result of decisions by man; this is common sense.

Our liberty comes through our ability to choose freely. But in choosing freely God also permits us to reap the consequences of our decisions, either, right or wrong, good and bad. People have never experienced liberty when oppressed, only in the freedom of choice. People are not free under a dictatorship where everything is given to them. They are only free in a free-enterprise system of choices and decisions.

However, those decisions could have been made differently, which would have produced different results. This is God's plan of organization. This is God's love.

Let the last paragraph sink in a bit, because it will take us into the rest of this chapter and spin into the next couple. I believe and know deep in my heart a line must be drawn in leading people.

Just as God lets us drift, so we must let others drift. God lets us drift, and when He calls us to let us know we have gotten too far away it is up to us to get back. This is because God loves us. Sadly, some get angry at God because their choices let them drift away from our loving father. In reality they get angry with God because God loves us. They get insulted and refuse to respond to God. This is what Jesus dealt with in Mathew 23.

When we receive God's forgiveness and apply it to our heart, then and only then are we able to forgive others. When we experience forgiveness and the liberty we feel, then we can forgive others. This is exactly what a relationship with God is all about.

We cannot force our will and purposes upon people, in doing so we are abusing them. These acts are in contrary to the plan and organization, which God has instilled. While I am all for an organized life and every individual having organization in their individual day-to-day affairs; I am against organizing their lives for them or placing undue burdens on people.

It is a fact our lives as humans are directly influenced by our thoughts, emotions, and resulting decisions. We are wonderfully and individually made and constructed. Thoughts and emotions; it is part of what makes us humans, and distinguishes us from animals.

Some people are stronger in certain areas of life than others. Inevitably you will discover individuals who are stronger physically than yourself, while others seem to have a certain degree of mental and emotional strength. These strengths and weaknesses develop our decisions on a daily basis, which affect all we come into contact with.

All of us have friends, acquaintances, and even enemies, which we admire for their inner strength. We have coworkers or we know someone who tells us of others, which have exceeded expectations for themselves. We read magazine articles or watch the news and witness people who have beat the odds and conquered cancer and other diseases.

The opposite also holds true. Over the course of time you will no doubt have the opportunity to observe certain individuals who are weak in specific areas of their life. This is usually where abuse comes in. When weaker individuals are dominated by stronger ones, weaker individual usually have a strength the abuser is jealous of.

Often times this weakness has been caused by some sort of abuse, whether psychological, or from a Christian perspective, spiritual abuse. This happens when someone has forced their will, or another agenda upon them. Acknowledging others weakness represents the power of forgiveness. When we forgive others, we acknowledge the presence of God in us.

My born again experience really began when I was seventeen years of age and still living in Ohio. I attended a Catholic Renewal. I went to a day-long event where I was confronted with my own spirituality.

At this renewal we read from and shared through personal interaction what we believed and did not believe as individuals. In the afternoon a man came forward and began to share how he had grown into having a special personal relationship with God.

I cannot remember the specifics of what he said or did. One thing I do remember is once he finished we were given a space of alone time. I left, went down the hallway into a chapel, and began to pray and ask God to come into my heart and help me.

On this particular day, God touched my heart. I was different after this encounter. I experienced God's forgiveness and grace. I remember returning home and even my Mother saying I was different. It was a short time later while working at my first full time job I would hear a full explanation of coming into a personal relationship with God. Soon after this event I left for the Air Force.

The meat of my growing years was the 1970's. The 70s were ripe with religious extremists taking advantage of people and forcing their beliefs on them. Jim Jones, Rev Moon, the shepherding movement, and others taught and showed us the extreme side of spiritual and authoritarian abuse.

Spiritual Abuse occurs when a leader, belief system; whether religious or secular, or a church well intentioned or not, dominates, manipulates, or castigates individuals through fear tactics, mind control, or some other psychological or emotional abuse.

Spiritual abuse just does not stop there. It can be inflicted in day-to-day life and by those we would never suspect. Spiritual abuse I personally believe is the worst level of abuse that can be experienced by an individual. Jesus dealt with this in Mathew 23 when he confronted the Pharisees. The Pharisees were religious leaders in Jesus' day who would force things and events on the common person of which they would not do themselves.

When someone abuses you spiritually they are stripping you of your inner power and self-esteem. They are attacking your soul. They are inflicting huge hurt and trauma on your Core Value.

This can happen no matter the religion. Catholic, Protestant, Hindu, Muslim, it does not matter. It can be instigated by any form of religious authority. If religion is not involved it can be perpetrated by doctors, therapists, and counselors.

In my personal case, my ex-wife's counselor was wielding abuse on people. It becomes a real problem when one does it again and again damaging people as it goes on and on. The extreme problem is when they do it again and again and it goes on and on and the perpetrator thinks he is correct in his or her assumptions and everyone else is wrong.

When we allow ourselves to continue to be a victim of this level of abuse we are, in effect, handing over our power to the abuser. It becomes easier to give into the lie than it does to fight back. We give up our homes and move into caves and settle for living under trees like they did in the days of Gideon.

I believe with all my heart I have been able to endure the pain and betrayal I started experiencing at the age of 47 was because I experienced God's forgiveness and grace at the age of 17. God began something in my life then, which permitted me to forgive and walk forward 30 years later.

I believe the following scripture, which I will use to close this chapter, is right on board for me, and concerning my life. I have been discouraged and encouraged. I have experience fear to the point I thought I could hear the enemy laughing at me. I have experienced to love and presence of God to the point where I could feel Him sitting next to me and putting his arm around me. All of my collective experiences, trials, and subsequent decisions have led me to this point in life. My life is good and I am thankful to God for it. I regret nothing, which has happened to me and I am grateful to God for a rich life!

I leave you with the following passage as recorded in the book of Ephesians, Chapter 2, verses 8-10

"God saved you by his grace when you believed. You can't take credit for this; it is a gift from God. Salvation is not a reward for the good things we have done, so none of us can boast about it.
We are God's masterpiece. He has created us anew in Christ Jesus, so we can do the good things he planned for us long ago."

Chapter Eight
Breaking Traditional Mindsets

"Learn from yesterday, live for today, hope for tomorrow."
-Albert Einstein (1879-1955)

In the New Testament of the bible before he was the apostle
Paul who wrote half of the New Testament, he was Saul of Tarsus. Saul
was a Pharisee, and a strict one. Pharisee's attempted to live in a
constant state of purity, by both the Oral law and the Torah. We read in
the book of Acts how the new church and the believers in Jesus Christ
were experiencing a great time of growth.

They were witnessing miracles. Such miracles consisted of the
very shadow of the Apostle Peter passing over people, many were
healed. Lame people walking and Phillip being supernaturally
transported from one location to another. The book of Acts records the
following passage:

Acts 5:14-16

*"Yet more and more people believed and were brought to the Lord—
crowds of both men and women.* [15] *As a result of the apostles' work,
sick people were brought out into the streets on beds and mats so that
Peter's shadow might fall across some of them as he went by.* [16] *Crowds
came from the villages around Jerusalem, bringing their sick and those
possessed by evil spirits, and they were all healed."*

These and many other events led Saul to persecute the true
church and exercise a tight fisted control over the believers lives. It led
to the martyrdom of Stephen, recorded as the first martyr of the early
Christian church. This was after Stephen got in the Pharisees faces and
told them the truth.

Acts 7:54 – 59 states the following:

[54] *The Jewish leaders were infuriated by Stephen's accusation, and they
shook their fists at him in rage.* [55] *But Stephen, full of the Holy Spirit,
gazed steadily into heaven and saw the glory of God, and he saw Jesus
standing in the place of honor at God's right hand.* [56] *And he told them,
"Look, I see the heavens opened and the Son of Man standing in the
place of honor at God's right hand!"*

[57] *Then they put their hands over their ears and began shouting. They
rushed at him* [58] *and dragged him out of the city and began to stone
him. His accusers took off their coats and laid them at the feet of a
young man named Saul.*

*⁵⁹ as they stoned him, Stephen prayed, "Lord Jesus, receive my spirit."
⁶⁰ He fell to his knees, shouting, "Lord, don't charge them with this
sin!" And with that, he died.*

Verse 58 says, "They laid their coats at the feet of Saul," this
was an act of obedience in their culture, signifying they approved of
what Saul was doing. Saul wielded his authoritarian sword being in a
role of leadership among the Pharisees. The Pharisees were organized in
this way. This was their filing system. This did not mean the Pharisees
or Saul were correct and as we find out in Acts chapter nine, he was not.

Like I previously stated, I believe in organization and a proper
filing system. I do not however approve of this type of approach when it
comes to dealing with and treating people. We become slaves to our
Fear only because we let ourselves become slaves. We continue to
suffer abuse because we permit it to happen in our lives. The Jewish
followers of Saul succumbed to the fear Saul supplanted onto them.

Spiritual abuse is about someone taking control over another
person's mind, thoughts, creativity, and dreams. These are the things,
which motivate us in life and move us to strive toward good things for
ourselves, our family, and environment. In essence the spiritual abusers
attempt to "set up people to be filed in an organized way."

Spiritual abuse is about power and control, as all abuse is. It
seeks to dominate you, to manipulate you, in the end it renders you
incapable of making your own decisions. It puts you into a file; nice and
neatly to keep you until they need you.

It attempts to fold you into "6 inch squares" so you will fit into
their drawer. It opens the door to all other abuse including physical
abuse, sexual abuse, and spousal abuse.

If someone can destroy your spirit, then you become mentally impaired and paralyzed. You are unable to reason your decisions and thought processes. You begin to see and feel things, which are not there. "You begin to ignore the fact the abuse is undeserved treatment; therefore, depleting your self-esteem." [2]

I firmly believe nothing just happens. It is for a reason.

All the events of your life; good, bad, hard, easy, painful, betrayal, psychological abuse, sexual abuse, sickness, disease, and all the suffering, are for a reason!

Let this sink in for a bit. The reason is to bring you into a complete personal relationship with God. What I have just said will be thronged by many as nonsense and thrown out. People say, "How can God let all these bad things happen?"

It is part of Gods design, it is His plan. Nothing just happens! Only He completely knows us. Only He completely understands us. He knows exactly what it will take to get us to respond to his calling. It is sad but many reject him.

They may not understand what I just said. Many will at this point leave God and forsake him. This will usually happen right before the miracle, right before the break though.

Even the misguided actions of Saul were all part of God's plan. They were part of His plan for Saul, for the believers, and for Stephen. These actions brought about a stirring in the new church in Jerusalem. It caused the believers to scatter and leave and to take the Gospel message throughout the known world.

Hebrews 13: 5-6

Let your conduct be without covetousness; be content with such things as you have. For He Himself has said, "I will never leave you nor forsake you." [6] So we may boldly say:

"The LORD is my helper
I will not fear.
What can man do to me?"

I firmly believe there is nothing which can keep us from getting totally free from our circumstances. Low self esteem keeps us locked into unhealthy or toxic relationships with others. Being involved in a dominating, controlling church, marriage, and friendship is a toxic relationship. When we continue to allow ourselves to become spiritually abused, it is only a matter of time before this abuse becomes physical. Anger sets into our lives and we most always will vent the anger at the ones we love the most, and not at the one inducing the abuse onto us.

When we are abused (not sexually) by clergy or other "men of God" the abuse, which turns physical is never directed back at the abuser, it is almost always inflicted on those we love, mainly our immediate family members. In the case of the apostle Paul, The Lord stepped in and literally knocked Paul off of his horse.

Acts 9:1-9 Saul's conversion

[1] *Meanwhile, Saul was uttering threats with every breath and was eager to kill the Lord's followers. So he went to the high priest. [2] He requested letters addressed to the synagogues in Damascus, asking for their*

cooperation in the arrest of any followers of the Way he found there. He wanted to bring them—both men and women—back to Jerusalem in chains.

³ As he was approaching Damascus on this mission, a light from heaven suddenly shone down around him. ⁴ He fell to the ground and heard a voice saying to him, "Saul! Saul! Why are you persecuting me?"

*⁵ **"Who are you, lord?"** Saul asked.*

And the voice replied, "I am Jesus, the one you are persecuting! ⁶ Now get up and go into the city, and you will be told what you must do."

⁷ The men with Saul stood speechless, for they heard the sound of someone's voice but saw no one!⁸ Saul picked himself up off the ground, but when he opened his eyes he was blind. So his companions led him by the hand to Damascus. ⁹ He remained there blind for three days and did not eat or drink.

After the crucifixion and resurrection of Jesus, mans relationship with God changed because not only of these, but because of the shed blood of Jesus. Once Jesus ascended into heaven he became our advocate with Father God.

Jesus said to Saul, "Why do you persecute me?"

From this day forward anything we do to anybody in any way, affects the Lord himself. If we abuse others, we are abusing the Lord himself. Also notice in verse 5, Saul uses the word lord with a small "l" since Saul was not fully converted yet.

Painful relationships whether professional or intimate develop for many reasons. Sadly, there are times when people hurt people out of meanness; they intentionally use, abuse, and damage the other person.

At the same time, many harmful, toxic interactions have nothing to do with the desire to cause pain; they are a reaction to the abuse we are under. Many times we don't even realize we are being dominated and controlled spiritually. The troubles may be largely due to a person's own emotional wounding, stressful lifestyle, mental illness, or addiction to alcohol and other drugs.

Spiritual abuse is the most challenging form of abuse to heal from. The wounds from a physical abuse will heal in time but healing from spiritual abuse takes tremendous effort on the part of the survivor to overcome.

In this story of the Apostle Paul there was a key ingredient in his conversion. This ingredient was not in the control of Paul's hands or decision, but in the decision of another.

This is precisely what I have mentioned prior to this chapter. Our decisions matter in a way so that others will benefit. Others benefit with our decisions to be free from abuse. This is as profound in my life, as I have had to make difficult decisions to be free and go beyond the common thinking and prevalent mindset of others.

These decisions are not based on logic or a prevailing mindset. They are decisions in obedience. In my case and situation it was what I knew God himself wanted me to do. In closing we read on about Ananias and his reaction with his instruction from God concerning Paul and Paul's conversion.

Acts 9:10-19

[10] *Now there was a believer in Damascus named Ananias. The Lord spoke to him in a vision, calling, "Ananias!"*

"Yes, Lord!" he replied.

[11] *The Lord said, "Go over to Straight Street, to the house of Judas. When you get there, ask for a man from Tarsus named Saul. He is praying to me right now.* *[12]* *I have shown him a vision of a man named Ananias coming in and laying hands on him so he can see again."*

[13] *"But Lord," exclaimed Ananias, "I've heard many people talk about the terrible things this man has done to the believers in Jerusalem!* *[14]* *And he is authorized by the leading priests to arrest everyone who calls upon your name."*

[15] *But the Lord said, "Go, for Saul is my chosen instrument to take my message to the Gentiles and to kings, as well as to the people of Israel.* *[16]* *And I will show him how much he must suffer for my name's sake."*

[17] *So Ananias went and found Saul. He laid his hands on him and said, "Brother Saul, the Lord Jesus, who appeared to you on the road, has sent me so that you might regain your sight and be filled with the Holy Spirit."* *[18]* *Instantly something like scales fell from Saul's eyes, and he regained his sight. Then he got up and was baptized.* *[19]* *Afterward he ate some food and regained his strength.*

Saul of Tarsus was converted this day to Christianity and became the Apostle Paul. Ananias's decision to obey God and deny the abuse he suffered at the hands of Saul, whether directly or indirectly, and go against the prevailing mindset, set Saul free to become Paul. This act of obedience set in motion the conversion of millions of people over the next 2 millennium.

This thought is staggering. The results of one decision go way beyond what Ananias ever thought or dreamed about. How much further can our decision go if we choose to change and shed our abuses? How many people benefit when we choose to no longer be a victim, but choose to be a survivor? We must choose to be a miracle to others.

The survivor must completely reprogram his or her life to build a new self worth and inner strength, which will prevent them from ever becoming a victim to spiritual abuse again. Ananias did this when he went and prayed for Saul to receive his sight. On this day in scripture Ananias chose to reprogram his thinking, and his mindset.

So how does all this fit into transitioning into a survivor from being a victim? Understanding you are being abused is a key step to recovery. The other side is those whom have been abused without their knowledge, will almost always tend to abuse others. Most do not even realize they have been abused and are abusing and or controlling others. This was the case of Saul. Yet, this was all part of God's plan. None of these recorded stories happened by chance.

Remember,

<u>Nothing just happens, it is all for a reason. It all has a purpose.</u>

Notes Chapter 8

[1] New Living Translation of the Bible, Thomas Nelson publishers

[2] http://www.spiritual-research network.com spiritualabuse.html.
Retrieved January 12, 2011

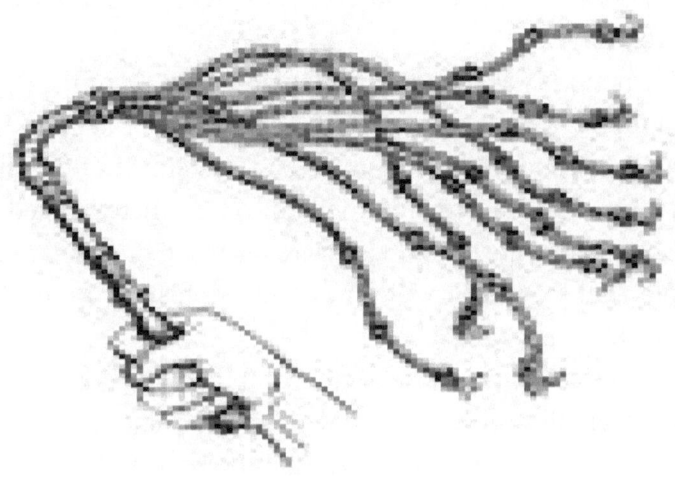

Chapter Nine:
Modern Day Scribes, Pharisees, and Hypocrites

"Evil men prevail when the righteous do not speak out against injustice."

John Huss (Jan Hus) was born in Bohemia (now part of the Czech Republic) in about 1371. He received a master's degree from Charles University in Prague in 1396. He became a professor of theology in 1398, and was ordained to the priesthood in 1400. He was made rector of the University in 1402. In 1404 He received a bachelor's degree in theology (presumably a more advanced degree than the term suggests today).

In Huss's day there was a crisis of authority in the Western Catholic Church. In 1305, under pressure from the King of France, the seat of the Popes was moved from Rome to Avignon in France where it remained for 70 years.

This period is called the Babylonian Captivity of the Papacy, suggesting the 70 years Jerusalem lay desolate after when the Jews were deported to Babylon as recorded in the Old Testament of the Bible.

In 1376 the then pope returned to Rome, where he died soon after. The cardinals, mostly French, were disposed or called to elect a French Pope, but the people of Rome objected, fearing a French Pope would move the Papacy back to France.

The cardinals therefore elected an Italian Pope, and then fled elsewhere, where they elected a French Pope and said the first election had been under duress, and was void. Thus there were two (later three) claimants for the Papal Office.

The Council of Constance was called to settle the matter. One claimant recognized the validity of the Council, but then abdicated and changed his mind. The Council responded by proclaiming he had been the true Pope. It then deposed the other two, and elected a new Pope, thus healing the schism.

Meanwhile, Huss had begun to denounce various church abuses in his sermons. His disputes with authority did not concern basic theological issues, but rather matters of church discipline and practice. The custom had arisen, at celebrations of the Lord's Supper, of distributing the consecrated bread to all Christians in good standing who desired to receive it, but restricting the chalice to the priest alone. This basically meant everyone could eat the bread, but only the priest or pastor could drink the wine.

Huss denounced this restriction as contrary to Holy Scripture and to the ancient tradition of the Church. He also held the belief church officials ought to exercise spiritual powers only, and not be earthly governors. In 1412 his archbishop excommunicated him, not for heresy, but for insubordination. The real problem was Huss supported one papal claimant and the archbishop another. Huss's candidate was ultimately declared to be the true pope.

These matters came to a head when one claimant (later declared unfit) proclaimed a sale of indulgences to raise money for a war against his rivals. (Indulgences are when the church takes people's money, thus telling them the indulgence will save their dead loved one from hell and promises they will be in heaven.)

Huss was horrified at the idea of selling spiritual benefits to finance a war between two claimants to the title "Servant of the Servants of God," and said so to all involved.

In 1414 Huss was summoned to the Council of Constance, with the Emperor guaranteeing his personal safety even if found guilty. Huss was tried, and ordered to recant certain heretical doctrines. Huss replied he had never held or taught the doctrines in question, and was willing to declare the doctrines false, but not willing to declare on oath he had once taught them.

The one point on which Huss could be said to have a doctrinal difference with the Council was he taught the office of the pope did not exist by Divine command, but was established by the Church (people), in which things might be done in an orderly fashion (a view he shared with Thomas Moore).

The Council, having just narrowly succeeded in uniting Western Christendom (Catholicism) under a single pope after years of chaos, was not about to have its work undone. It accordingly found Huss guilty of heresy, and he was burned at the stake on July 6, 1415.

After Huss's death, his followers continued to insist on the importance of administering the Holy Communion in kinds, (wine &

bread) and defeated several armies sent against them. In 1436 a pact was signed, by which the Church in Bohemia was authorized to administer Chalice (wine) as well as Host (bread) to all communicants.

The followers of John Huss and his fellow martyr Jerome of Prague became known as the Czech Brethren and later as the Moravians. The Moravian Church survives to this day.

The Moravian church had a considerable influence on the Lutheran movement. When Martin Luther suddenly became famous after the publication of his 95 Theses, cartoons and graffiti began to appear implying Luther was the spiritual heir of John Huss.

When Martin Luther encountered the Pope's representative Johannes Eck, in a crucial debate, Eck sidestepped the questions of indulgences (paying money to the church so dead family members could be forgiven and not go to hell) and of justification by faith (salvation not by works), and instead asked Luther whether the Church had been right to condemn Huss.

When Luther, after thinking it over, said Huss had been unjustly condemned, the whole question of the authority of Popes and Councils was raised. [1]

If you are not Catholic, or were not raised Catholic you might not understand this story. Basically, Jon Huss wanted all people to receive the bread and wine in communion at church. Jon Huss suffered, was abused all for a reason. This very reason gave rise and began the Protestant revolution of the known church by way of Martin Luther.

John Huss stood up against the religious hierarchy of his day, and refused to back down. He refused to agree to things, in which he did not say or do. Today this story seams so small, but In Jon Huss's day, this was a miracle! The church of that day sought to control Huss's teaching.

Today, I have many friends whom I have limited contact with who were involved with me in the early 80s through the 1990s. These were the early years of my born-again experience. Most if not all of these men and women who are still functioning in some sort of religious ministry have all told me point blank, "they want nothing to do with the men who were in authority over us as individuals," during that particular period.

These men (my friends) claim to be called by God as pastors because our leaders said we were called by God. Wherein, like Hus we all claimed and knew the common person chose us for our authority as pastors. Yet, most if not all of these men continue and function the same way as our teachers did. They emphatically deny they are like our leaders. They dismiss my opinion when I tell them they are like our leaders and say I am an unbeliever.

They conduct their church business as our leaders did, whom we say are wrong. I am standing on the outside looking at it and I can see it, but they cannot! In essence they have become what they grew to despise the most! We all were spiritually abused and made to do things we did not want to do in the name of God.

We were never looked at as unique individuals. Our leadership in our young developing years for ministry never tapped our individual gifting. We were never given the chance to excel in our gifts; rather, we were programmed to be like our leadership. My friends hate and despise how they were treated, yet they now do the same and abuse others in the same fashion, and they do not even realize they are doing it!

Sadly, the mask of spiritual abuse deception can be worn by anyone. Including but not limited to spiritual systems, churches, unbiblical and biblical authority structures and of course, cults.

Even the philosophy and ideology of large and small
corporations can inflict spiritual or psychological abuse on individuals.
Doctors, therapists, and counselors can also be perpetrators of spiritual
abuse and psychological abuse.

William Enroth wrote a masterpiece named "churches that
abuse." Some of the men in control of these churches know exactly
what they want. Others can't see it and have been conditioned to accept
this behavior as acceptable in the eyes of God, and their own individual
organization.

All forms of spiritual abuse inevitably lead back to the one who
is the abuser; and most often it is the leader of the group. In almost all
cases the leader was abused in some way and never dealt with it, but
just buried it. I believe this is the case with the man my ex-wife sought
counsel from. He stated once to me how he despised the way churches
were organized. He detested organized religion. He abhorred leaders for
what they do to the people, but this is what he did to others.

Through his counseling this is exactly how he parlayed himself
to my ex-wife. When he confronted my ex-wife with her issues, she
buried her hurts and resentments. She then turned on me, the very
person who loved her most! He counseled her in the things he despised,
so in turn, she accused me of the very things which she buried in her
mind and despised.

Over the past three years I have spoken with Licensed Social
Workers, Licensed Psychotherapists, Psychology Instructors at school,
and my Psychiatrist. All of them unanimously and without any
knowledge I had spoken with any of the others have told me this type of
individual was probably abused as a child and probably by a person of
Clergy. These are the very things he accused me of, and retaliated
against me through my ex-wife and children.

Authoritarian abuse can simply be defined as a misuse and over emphasis on authority. Most if not all of these women or men have come from a history of abuse in their own individual lives. I believe this to be the case with my ex-wife's unlicensed counselor.

An individual can be spiritually abused by their employers or bosses. If someone strips you of your self-worth, makes you feel inadequate in your position, belittles or berates you, then you are suffering from spiritual abuse. Whatever an employer's intentions are, if you begin to feel belittled, then you are beginning to feel the effects of abuse. Spiritual abuse is just not suffered by those in religious systems. Spiritual abuse happens if your self-worth is threatened, weakened, or berated because it attacks your Core Value, which is your soul.

Abusive systems, which are religious in nature claim they are 'led by God' and therefore justify their 'abusive behavior' by saying they are 'God's leaders', etc.

This was the case when my ex-wife came under the therapy of a mad man counselor. On one occasion he boasted to me how he was doing a work for God and if he was incorrect in his teachings over the years, then God himself would stop him. My ex-wife put a validation stamp on this statement and others this counselor made.

Abusive leaders, which include bad therapist, damage people in countless ways. "Recovering from spiritual abuse is a very painful process. Most people, who have never been abused spiritually or psychologically etc., do not understand what recovering from spiritual abuse is like. Sadly, most people assume once a person leaves an abusive system, group, leader, or workplace the problem is over." [1]

The following are common characteristics of being in a spiritually abusive system and of a spiritually abusive leader. I am stating here my views coming from a Christian perspective:

#1) Authoritarian – Matthew 23:4.
"You religious leaders crush people with unbearable religious demands; you never lift a finger to ease their burden."

The most distinctive characteristic of a spiritually abusive religious system, or leader, is the over-emphasis on authority. Because a group claims to have been established by God, the leaders in this system claim the right to command their followers.

In Matthew 23:12 Jesus said the Scribes and Pharisees "sit in Moses' seat," a position of spiritual authority. Many names are used but in the abusive system this is a position of power, not moral authority. The assumption is God operates among His people through a hierarchy, or "chain of command."

In this abusive system, unconditional submission is often called a "covering," or "umbrella of protection" which will provide some spiritual blessing to those who fully submit. Followers may be told God will bless their submission even if the leadership is wrong. It is not their place to judge or correct the leadership - God will see to this.

Individuality is also stripped from the individual. Most times in these cases the response from the leader will be "You can't have this idea by yourself. If your idea is truly from God, then surely I would have had the same idea since I am the leader."

This is what John Hus proclaimed when he cried out, "The office of the Pope (pastor) is not divinely given, but given by the will and choice of the common people"

#2 Image Conscious – Matthew 23:5-7

"Everything they do is for show. On their arms they wear extra wide prayer boxes with Scripture verses inside, and they wear robes with extra long tassels. They love to sit at the head table at banquets and in the seats of honor in the synagogues. ⁷ They love to receive respectful greetings as they walk in the marketplaces and to be called 'Rabbi.'"

The abusive religious system is scrupulous to maintain an image of righteousness. The organization's history is often misrepresented in the effort to demonstrate the organization's special relationship to God.

The mistaken judgments and character flaws of its leaders are denied or covered up to validate their authority. Impossibly high legalistic standards of thought and behavior may be imposed on the members. The member's failure to live up to these standards is a constant reminder of the member's inferiority to the leaders, and the necessity of submission to them. Abusive religion is, at heart, legalism.

Abusive religion or legalism is also paranoid. Because the truth about the abusive religious system would be quickly rejected if recognized; outsiders are shown only a positive image of the group. This is rationalized by assuming the religion would not be understood by "worldly" people; therefore they have no right to know.

This attitude leads to members being secretive about some doctrines and the inner policies and procedures of the group. Leaders, especially, will keep secrets from their members. This secrecy is rooted in a basic distrust of others because the belief system is false and cannot stand scrutiny.

#3 Suppresses Criticism- Matthew 23:31-33

"But in saying that, you testify against yourselves that you are indeed the descendants of those who murdered the prophets. [32] Go ahead and finish what your ancestors started. [33] Snakes! Sons of vipers! How will you escape the judgment of hell?"

Because the religious system is not based on the truth it cannot allow questions, dissent, or open discussions about issues. The person who dissents becomes the problem rather than the issue he raised. The truth about any issue is settled and handed down from the top of the hierarchy.

Questioning anything is considered a challenge to authority. Thinking for oneself is suppressed by pointing out it leads to doubts. This is portrayed as unbelief in God and His anointed leaders. Thus the follower controls his own thoughts by fear of doubting God. If individuals in the system were to be independently successful with views other than the authorities, they are quickly suppressed or chased away as to not "infect" other members.

This happened personally to me when I first moved to Albany, Oregon. I was associated in a church and was permitted to teach a bible study. I did not have a lesson plan or any structure to this bible study. What we did was read the bible and then every couple of read verses we would stop and have discussion.

This bible study became really popular and in time everyone came to this bible study and the other bible studies in the church were vacant, including the one taught by the pastor himself.

The pastor called me into his office one day and wanted me to explain my lesson plan. I told him I did not have one, except for what I was doing. This was actually letting the "common people" dictate how the bible study proceeded.

All I did was kept it on course. The pastor then stated to me,

"I cannot deny the success of your bible study, but I do not believe you can have this idea alone. I need to keep structure to everything we do in this church. Since I am the leader and in authority by God, surely I would have had the same idea."

The pastor and his wife soon thereafter closed and terminated my bible study completely. They stopped it and told everybody I was not teaching anymore. Instead of utilizing the success of my decisions, he and she felt I was a threat to their "God given authority." Soon thereafter we were asked to leave the church completely.

What is really interesting about this scenario are these pastors wanted me to be involved with leadership. I asked them,

"What do you want me to do?"

They told me to think of something, but when they told me this, I believe they really did not think I would be a success. When the bible study turned out to be a success, then they were offended because they did not come up with the idea. This threatened there authority. So they ran me out!

#4 Perfectionists – Matthew 23:25-26

"What sorrow awaits you teachers of religious law and you Pharisees? Hypocrites! For you are so careful to clean the outside of the cup and the dish, but inside you are filthy—full of greed and self-indulgence! ²⁶You blind Pharisee! First wash the inside of the cup and the dish, and then the outside will become clean, also."

A most natural assumption is a person does not get something for nothing. Apart from the Christian expression declaring "Salvation is by grace through faith, which God has given in the scriptures," it would be natural to think one must earn salvation, or at least work to keep it.

Thus, in abusive religions all blessings come through performance of spiritual requirements. Failure is strongly condemned so there is only one alternative, which is of perfection. So long as the follower thinks he or she is succeeding in his or her observation of the rules, the follower typically exhibits pride, elitism, and arrogance.

However, when reality and failure eventually set in, the result is the person experiences spiritual burnout, or even shipwreck of his faith and life. Those who fail in their efforts are labeled as apostates, weak, or some other such term so they can be discarded by the system.

#5 Unbalanced Teaching - Matthew 23: 23-24

"What sorrow awaits you teachers of religious law and you Pharisees? Hypocrites! You are careful to tithe even the tiniest income from your herb gardens, but you ignore the more important aspects of the law— justice, mercy, and faith. You should tithe, yes, but do not neglect the more important things. [24] Blind guides! You strain your water so you won't accidentally swallow a gnat, but you swallow a camel instead."

Abusive religions must distinguish themselves from all other religions so they can claim to be distinctive and therefore special to God. This is usually done by majoring on minor issues such as prophecy, carrying biblical law to extremes, or using strange methods of biblical interpretation. The imbalanced spiritual hobby-horse thus produced, represents unique knowledge or practices which seem to validate the group's claim to special status with God.

I believe every setback in life can be conquered. I believe we can change. I believe we can be free, and the effects will no longer seek to control our heart, mind, and soul. If our focus is placed upon the opportunity to get stronger as a result of our failure and weakness instead of how weak we are because of our failure or weakness, then there is no mountain we cannot conquer in life.

I empathize with those who are suffering and trying to become free from spiritual abusers. It is my whole reason and motivation for writing this book. It is my hope my recovering from spiritual and emotional abuse can be of help to any and all who are reading this.

The Bible, once misinterpreted, quickly becomes the most abused book in the world. Scripture abuse includes inaccurate quotations, twisted translations, ignoring the immediate context of Scripture, and reading into a text what is not there. These abuses (perversions) of Scripture or other religious text form the vast and subtle religious text twisting justifications of spiritual abusers.

This is the basis for the terrorism in our world. It is true the abuse of Scripture and other religious text is the foundation of a religious leader's deceit. Don't be fooled by those who would supplant [to supersede (another) especially by force or treachery] your eternity through Scripture or other religious text abuse. [2]

Looking from the outside, it can be difficult to fully understand the severity of the psychological or spiritual abuse and how deeply it affects us as individuals. In my life men in authority had their effects on me. The most damaging and hurtful experience I had was watching and listening as my own family tried to speak and wield the lies supplanted in their minds by bad therapy through Marion Knox.

Even if you are experienced and trained in dealing with these kinds of situations, the answers can still be confusing and puzzling as to the ramifications this type of men parlay into social problems.

Many times people receive psychological abuse from their very own family members; in my case I feel the psychological abuse started when I became separated from my family at their own hand.

<u>When this is the case, often, the victim feels as though they have no choice and no option.</u>

I felt totally helpless in dealing with my own family members. Numbness creeps into your mind, heart and soul. It is as if all your strength is drained in just keeping your sanity and combating the ideologies of men like Knox. Instead I began to feel trapped by my circumstances.

When this happened I began experiencing the psychological abuse stemming from Knox and felt as though I had no way to prevent this kind of behavior on my part and was left without an adequate defense.

<u>Shannon Cook lists these 6 signs if you have been psychologically or spiritually abused, whether you are female or male.</u>

1. You are put down verbally, in public and or private. These putdowns may be blatant or more subtle, but they all add up to make you feel worthless, inferior, or immoral. The individual uses this technique to make you feel powerless and dependant, and create the illusion they are superior.

2. An individual withholds or demands physical intimacy. (Intimacy is not limited to sex) If your partner denies you intimacy deliberately or demands you fulfill their desires, regardless of your state of being, this is an emotionally abusive tactic. Both the denial and the demand hold's you hostage and communicates your wishes and needs are irrelevant and not as important as the abuser's wants and needs.

3. There is an attempt on the individual's part to control your activities. If the individual demands an account of your daily activities, or puts pressure on you to only do certain "approved" things. This is a sign you are being emotionally abused.

4. An individual limits or attempts to limit your contact with family and friends. Isolation is a powerful technique for an abuser because it prevents you from getting outside perspective on what is going on in your life. If this individual gets upset or angry when you spend time with others, this indicates an abusive situation.

5. The individual implies non-physical punishment or threats if you do not comply with their demands and desires. Conversely, the individual may occasionally offer a kindness as a reward to keep you invested in the possibility your relationship with them can improve and can change.

6. You feel crazy, inferior, less intelligent, or question reality because of the things the individual says about you. For an abuser, keeping you off balance and feeling depressed and worthless ensures you will continue to feel dependent and under their control. [4]

Shannon Cook is a personal growth and relationship expert who has written a number of informative articles and e-books on the topic of toxic relationships and holistic personal growth, including physical, emotional and relationship health.

For Christians, examples of spiritual abuse are found throughout the Bible [A]. Time does heal most wounds. The first step is realizing you are suffering from or being abused spiritually by church based clergy or psychologically by anyone outside of a church setting. Once you realize this you must decide to be free from it or it will take you down a long hill of devastation and shipwreck, **and with it bring abuse.**

It will affect your children and even your grandchildren.

You must recognize the perpetrator for who he or she is. If you fail to recognize the perpetrator for who he or she is, you will never begin to get free from the hold he, she, or it will have upon your life. If your views differ from those who you attempt to receive emotional support from, how do you think or believe this source will be able to help you? They never will. The first step to healing is recognizing the perpetrator, admitting what they did to you, and then decide you are going to do all in your power to recover and better your life.

Spiritual abuse has a devastating effect on people. A very high level of trust is often placed in spiritual leaders. It is, and ought to be, expected this trust will be honored and guarded. When such trust is violated the wound is very deep.

Sometimes the wound is so deep the wounded person cannot trust even a legitimate spiritual authority again. [3] This is what I want to see in others, the ability to see the perpetrator for who they are and the victim can and will be able to trust again.

The main symptom is the inability to relate normally to people who represent the source of their emotional injury. Besides an unhealthy fear of, and disillusionment with, spiritual authorities, the spiritually abused person may find it difficult to trust even God.

You say to yourself,

"How could (or why did) God let this happen to me?"

Anger is also deeply felt. Anger itself is not always wrong - God Himself expresses anger at such spiritual abuse (see Biblical Response, above). However, even legitimate anger, if not properly channeled and dealt with, can degenerate into bitterness and cynicism toward everything spiritual. This is why you must realize, God permits everything to happen for a reason. This can be difficult to accept. But once you do, then you are on a path of healing and recovery.

When an individual is involved in a spiritually abuse system coupled with receiving counseling or therapy in the same atmosphere, then their lives can become volatile and toxic. In most cases they cover up their deep rooted hurt from the abuse and coat it with "good works."

Sadly and eventually the underlying hurts will crumble and all the things built upon them will fall with it. In these circumstances loved ones are almost always hurt, relationships damaged, and catastrophe is the result. I do not believe all things magically disappear with salvation. I believe with salvation we are restored and renewed. It is then this combination with our efforts, will lead to healing the hurts with the blood of Jesus applied at salvation.

Jesus often told those he prayed for "go and sin no more, less a worse thing comes upon you." It takes effort and the guidance of a loving leader to lead those who have been hurt to a place where only the miracle of the Cross can do the healing and bring restoration and not to control and manipulate.

Notes Chapter 7, 8 &9

[A] For Christians, examples of spiritual abuse are found throughout the Bible. God describes (and condemns) the "shepherds of Israel" who feed themselves rather than the flock. God also describes those who do not heal those who are hurting, or seek to bring back those who were driven away, but rather discard them, ruling with force and cruelty (Ezekiel 34:1-10).

Jesus reacted with anger against the thievery of the money changers in the Temple as they misused God's people for selfish reasons (Matthew 21:12-13; Mark 11:15-18; Luke 19:45-47; John 2:13-16). He was angry at those more concerned with rules and regulations than with human suffering (Mark 3:1-5).

In John chapter 9, the Pharisees "cast out" the man born blind simply because the truth he told about his healing exposed their own corruption.

In Acts 7:51-56, Stephen called the Jewish leaders into account over their spiritual abuse. His testimony of Christ vindicated Jesus, whom they had abused, and Stephen condemned them for this. The legalistic Jews were so angry they stoned Stephen to death.

In Galatians Paul addresses a performance based Christianity, which leads to the abuse known as legalism. There are many more such examples. Jesus had legitimate spiritual authority, which was given to him by God. But, He did not exercise it to gain power for Himself, or to abuse and control others with rules and regulations.

Jesus said, "Come unto me all ye who labor and are heavy laden and I will give you rest" (Matt. 11:28). The Greek word for "heavy laden" is *phortizo,* which means here "to *overburden* with ceremony (or spiritual anxiety)" (*Strong's Concordance* #5412). [2]

Jesus gave a balanced perspective on positional authority when he said, "But, be not ye called Rabbi: for one is your Master, even Christ; and all ye are brethren" (Matthew 23:8). He gave another key to discernment when He taught, "He that speaks of himself seeks his own glory." (John 7:18a).

Jesus was not "image conscious." He was willing to associate with wine drinkers, cheating tax collectors and even prostitutes. He accused the legalistic Pharisees of "teaching for doctrine the commandments of men" (Matthew 15:9) and likened their showy, hypocritical outward righteousness to "whited sepulchers, which indeed appear beautiful outwardly, but are within full of dead men's bones, and of all uncleanness" (Matthew 23:27).

Neither was He paranoid. His ministry was conspicuously open to the public. When He was on trial (John 18) He was asked about His teachings and His reply was, "Why ask thou me?" Jesus pointed out He always taught in public, and never in secret, so why not ask His disciples. Jesus had nothing to hide.

Jesus did not fear to criticize the religious leaders or their faulty doctrines (e.g. Matthew 15:1-9; 23:1-39, etc.). And when confronted with criticism or with treacherous questions designed to discredit Him, His response was never to simply demand silence or only positive recognition from His accusers. Rather, He gave answers - scriptural and reasonable answers - to their objections (e.g. Luke 7:36-47; Matthew 19:3-9). Jesus upheld the high standard of the Law, yet He clearly placed the legitimate needs of people before any rules or regulations (Matthew 12:1-13; Mark 2:23-3:5).

The scriptures make it clear, no one will cease to sin in this life (Ecclesiastes 7:20; 1 John 1:8). Jesus made it plain, however, one can know in this life they can have eternal life (John 5:24; 6:37-40), a theme developed by Paul throughout his epistles, and by John (1 John 5:10-13).

The Pharisees, quintessential spiritually abusive leaders, were quite unbalanced in their perception of what mattered most to God. Jesus said they, "pay tithe of mint and anise and cumin, and have omitted the weightier matters of the law, - judgment, mercy, and faith" (Matthew23:23).

[1] http://justus.anglican.org/resources/bio/7.html

[2] http://www.spiritual-research network.com/spiritualabuse.html. Retrieved January 12, 201

 [3] Kovabis Jones, 2010 Retrieved January 14, 2011 from http://www.helium.com

[4] http://EzineArticles.com/?expert=Shannon_E_Cook

Chapter Ten:
The Poverty of the West

"There is more hunger in the world for love and appreciation than for bread"- Mother Theresa

In 1979, Mother Teresa was awarded the Nobel Peace Prize. This was for her work undertaken in the struggle to overcome poverty and distress, which also constitutes a threat to peace. Mother Teresa refused the conventional ceremonial banquet given to laureates, and asked the $192,000 in funds be given to the poor in India, stating,

"Earthly rewards were important only if they helped her help the worlds needy."

When Mother Teresa received the prize, she was asked, "What can we do to promote world peace?" She answered

"Go home and love your family."

Building on this theme in her Nobel Lecture, Mother Teresa said:

"Around the world and not only in the poor countries, I discovered the poverty of the West so much more difficult to remove. When I pick up a person from the street in India who is hungry, I give him a plate of rice, a piece of bread, and I have satisfied them, I have removed the hunger. But a person, which is shut out, which feels unwanted, unloved, and terrified; this person, which has been thrown out from society. It is this type of poverty, which is so hurt-able and so much more moving; I find this to be very difficult."

Mother Teresa dedicated her life to reaching hurting and abused people. She went to them and attempted to comfort them. She fed them and gave them a place to live and sleep.

What she then referred to as "the poverty of the west", (sexual abuse, emotion, and psychological abuse) she had no answers except to say "Go and love your family." This is how I will attempt to complete this book, about Love. Unconditional love; my attempts will be feeble. All I can do is share what I have learned through these past experiences and forms of abuse I have lived through during my lifetime. Love is why Jesus gave his life for us. Love will be the vehicle by which you heal on your journey to becoming a survivor, and then a victor!

It is this type of poverty, which goes beyond human understanding, which Mother Teresa was speaking of. Our hurt, which we suffer at first, puts us in a desert place. It is up to us to journey out of the desert place and to a place or area where we can let our hurt heal.

We must assume there will be nobody there to help us. Placing hope in someone else can only lead to further hurt and devastation if they are not able to help us. This journey from our desert place can only be determined by us. Your journey can only be determined by you! We reach this determination differently and in our own ways.

It is at this point where I want to begin to speak of the incredible and overwhelming peace, contentment, and freedom, which flooded my soul very soon after my personal ordeal begun.

I was speaking to a friend recently and she asked me about the peace I kept speaking about and what I was experiencing in my life. I told her I would try, but my worldly definition would be an insult and an injustice to the true meaning of the peace.

<u>Truly from God</u>

I told her, "It's hard to put into words and put a definition on it because it was truly from God himself. God resides in heaven. It is a piece of heaven, this peace I am experiencing."

I went on to say, "the word peace as we know it and how our dictionaries define, is no comparison to what I am experiencing." She told me she thought she understood. She then went on to tell me she could tell when it was on me because as she put it, "You look different."

This has been the comment I have heard from people when the peace, as the bible describes in Philippians 4:7, comes over me,

<u>"Then you will experience God's peace, which exceeds anything we can understand. His peace will guard your hearts and minds as you live in Christ Jesus."</u>

It was recently I visited with friends whom I had not seen in quite some years. Sitting there and speaking to them, they said later they could feel the peace I was speaking of. Later in a telephone conversation she said to me,

"I don't know how all of this drama will play out in your life Steve, but I can see the Lord is in control of your life"

She went on to say,

"I was praying for you and for reconciliation with your marriage when I just could not pray, I was confused. I felt like I ran into a brick wall. It was like a huge weight on me. So I stopped and just began to pray for you and this overwhelming peace came over me. It was so strong I had to telephone you to tell you."

Many people have told me this. I believe it is the ones who really hear from God. My co-author in my first book told me the same. She said,

"At first when I heard your story I was really taken back and freaked out. But when I went home and slept and awoke the next morning, I had this incredible peace over my life. I just knew you were speaking the truth. I knew I wanted to help you in any way I could."

This peace is God's love. In the previous chapter of this book I attempted to fully explain my feelings concerning the abusive world we live in, and the abuses many endure even in a church setting. I have read it over and reread it. It is a bit dry. Then I thought this may be good, because the abuse, abusive leaders, and the desert journey we travel, are dry.

The pain of yesterday is the strength for today

I believe the greatest thing we face after being deeply hurt is an extremely vulnerable place once we emerge from the desert. The problem is most often we develop a place of comfort, once we have emerged. We find ourselves no longer there in the desert. The anger, bitterness, and resentment do not affect us as much as it did at one time.

It is good to have a place of comfort, a refuge so to say.

What we must be careful of is this place where we are when we emerge is solid ground (healed) and not temporary, (like a scab). We have to watch, lest the scab gets torn off prematurely and the open sore or wound, are not exposed again.

Our hurt, our vulnerability becomes the clay of choice in the hands of the Lord, the Master Potter of our lives. It is through this hurt and vulnerability, which God molds and refashions our life, if we let him. God prepares yesterdays pain as the foundation for the mortar to hold the bricks of our new life in place today.

Mother Teresa saw the hurt, abuse, and suffering in the world. It was through love, which she attempted to demonstrate the love of God to suffering humanity. My friend, it is love, which will lead you past your hurt, anguish, and abuse to a place of restoration where the Lord is the Master Potter.

I truly believe nothing just happens. Everything happens for a purpose and a reason.

<u>Isaiah 55: 8-9</u>
"My thoughts are nothing like your thoughts," says the LORD,
"and my ways are far beyond anything you could imagine; for just as
the heavens are higher than the earth, so my ways are higher than your
way and my thoughts higher than your thoughts.

It is the condition of our hearts, which leads us to react when these things happen in our life, whether good or bad. God says, His ways are not our ways. This is where we have to just trust God is in total control of all our circumstances.

Jesus spoke the following in the Gospel of Mathew, chapter 5, starting with verse 43,

"[43] "You have heard the law that says, 'Love your neighbor' and hate your enemy. [44] But I say, love your enemies! Pray for those who persecute you! [45] In that way, you will be acting as true children of your Father in heaven. For God gives his sunlight to both the evil person and the good, and He sends rain on the just person and the unjust alike. [46] If you love only those who love you, what reward is there for that? Even corrupt tax collectors do that much. [47] If you are kind only to your friends, how are you different from anyone else? Even pagans do that. [48] but you are to be perfect, even as your Father in heaven is perfect.

As a Christian, I believe God; through my faith in Jesus Christ is a restorer of my life. He is and can be the restorer of your shattered life. Every person born on this earth is unique. We have separate and distinct personalities.

This is why Jesus said what he said. What he was saying was God the father does not look down at us and make certain things happen because we are good or bad. They happen to each and every person the same.

When we feel God has been unjust or unfair with us or has favored others rather than us, it is yet another sign to us how far we have drifted from the Lord.

If God were to separate us, this would go contrary to His nature and character. (Even using this phrase is incorrect "His nature and His character") like we can define God, or understand what He is like.

I can only attempt to know and understand God because of His word. Slowly over time my focus changed from blaming others to an acceptance of my responsibility to heal and become an overcomer, a survivor.

The word survivor can tend to have negative connotations. However, being a survivor should only be a transitional stage in our lives. I believe we don't and should not remain a survivor forever. We all have unique lifestyles. Our collective beliefs and feelings associated with daily activity are unique. For example, each of us has two eyes, two ears, a nose, a mouth, a chin, and hair on our heads. We all have the same physical features, yet we all look different. God has created us all unique.

So also we have unique thoughts, feelings, and desires, which drive us. It is a logical assumption the outcomes of these thoughts, feelings, and desires cause a distinctive experience. These distinctive experiences will create their own set of outcomes.

This is why abuse and the resulting hurt we all experience is such a great injustice to us. What is more of an unfairness we cast upon ourselves is we all tend to wallow in our hurt resulting from these injustices. I personally believe our distinctive experiences are irreplaceable. They are a rare set of events placed in motion and exclusive to only us as individuals. In this manner I believe as Mother Teresa stated, "go home and love your family."

When I successfully won my hearing against the Oregon Department of Human Services (DHS); the war was far from being over. At first I believed this hearing was the war. After I defeated this foe, I soon discovered it was only a battle, a small skirmish, in the real war, which was waging against my life, mind, and soul.

My wife and children were still under the influence of the mad man named Marion Knox. His influence robbed me of the one basic thing, in which I wanted to do and this was "go home and love your family." I could not do this; no one permitted me to do this. Everyone kept me from doing this.

I do not hate the man Marion Knox, so please anything I may say is not to be construed as hate when I refer to him. The best way I can describe my feelings is I utterly disapprove of this man because of what he believes and teaches. His beliefs cause him to be arrogant, self centered, and insidious. His beliefs make him a sinister man. His beliefs leave him totally out of touch and off balance.

I will see the day this man stops his evil counseling and tearing apart of families. Mr. Knox thinks himself to be sagacious, clever, and perceptive, when in reality he is a very foolish man. I can only assume my family is still under his influence; dwelling on these thoughts too long leaves me dabbling with resentment.

I have found it is O.k. to get angry with God. Wow where did this comment come from along this train of thought? Over the past 3 years my frustration levels have peaked and receded. I have laid in bed for hours, crying due to the pain. Many times I just prayed for God to take my life. Over time I have found the pain to recede and an overwhelming peace to come over me.

In reading Regina Brett's book, "God Never Blinks" Ms. Brett tells a story about getting angry with God. The book is broken down into "50 lessons for Life's Little Detours." Lesson 8 is titled, "Its O.K. to get angry with God. He can take it!" Brett goes on to tell this story.

"I met Father Jim Lewis at the Jesuit Retreat House in Parma, Ohio. He was profound in his simplicity. He told me God wants a real, authentic, genuine relationship with us. The same kind of openness and honesty you have in a good marriage.

He discovered after struggling with a job transfer: he hated his new assignment. He tried holy obedience and acceptance, but he was miserable. He tried to pray with gratitude but didn't have any in him. He tried to play God's happy little servant, but it wasn't working.

Finally, one day he broke. He went to the chapel alone, greeted God and then softly cursed his holy heart out. "Damn, Damn, Damn, Damn." This was it. He said the same prayer every day until it was out of his system. Once the anger was gone, there was room for something else, Peace! The slate was clean. Now God could write on it. Father Lewis called it the 'Damn Prayer.'"

God wants more than us to have a close relationship with him. It is O.K. to get angry, yell, and even cuss in God's presence. He understands. He wants openness. He wants to see if we know we can come to him openly with no reservations into his presence and listening ear. When we can do this, the sky is the limit.

Our prayers in this atmosphere of openness will move mountains of opposition in our lives. Nothing is impossible to them who believe. He wants us to express ourselves as we are. He wants us to be us. Believe me my friend, HE KNOWS! He understands and knows my pain. He understands and knows your pain. Most of those who would scoff at these remarks are those who may very well have never needed God to lean on.

God knows our pain, He sees our hurt. He is right there with us as we travel the road to recovery and being a survivor. He is there listening, waiting, and wanting to step in and give us a miracle. I am truly grateful to God for all the miracles I have received. I don't know if I will ever be able to convey into words the hurt I suffered through and still deal with. There is an eternal tenderness left in my heart after my entire ordeal was inflicted on me. I APPRECIATE God so much for His faithfulness!

Sometimes the pain is so great, I do not know how I will make it through, yet I do. Then there are times I experience such a peace upon my life. There is such contentment in my heart, a great solitude. It is so peaceful I don't ever want to leave this intimate place, where God loves on me. I feel so close to God I feel as if I can reach out and touch him.

I have had moments when the pain was so intense and sharp my mind just becomes numb. Soon after these feelings overwhelm me I feel the presence of God come right next to me, as if He was sitting by my side. I have been driving in my car and have felt God's love and peace literally come and sit beside me as I drive. He has been so good to me through everything.

It is our painful places God is at work doing the most in our hearts. When we trust him, He begins to mend and fill the great empty spots left by those who have mocked me and abused me.

Many people are hurt in the passing of a loved one. In these times we feel alone and isolated. There is such a great emptiness in our lives, a void, which this person has left. In my circumstance the hardest thing to accept is the thought of never being able to reconcile with my former wife. Her decisions, however she may have arrived at them, have created a great emptiness.

The circumstances have left me with the thought and feeling my family was stolen from me. Sometimes I think it would have been better had a disaster taken all of their lives than to live through this circumstance. With each passing day, life becomes easier to handle. Like an ocean's tide, which comes in and goes out, so is my pain. At the same time as this tide in my life reacts, so does the strength. I realize this strength only does, and can come from The Lord himself.

The apostle Paul in the book of Philippians says these words,

"Now I want you to know and continue to rest assured, brethren, what has happened to me [this imprisonment] has actually only served to advance and give a renewed impetus to the [spreading of the] good news (the Gospel). So much is this a fact throughout the whole imperial guard and to all the rest [here] my imprisonment has become generally known to be in Christ. [I am a prisoner in His service and for Him]. And [also] most of the brethren have derived fresh confidence in the Lord because of my chains and are much bolder to speak and publish fearlessly the Word of God [acting with more freedom and indifference to the consequences]." Philippians 1:12-14 Amplified Bible

Nothing Just Happens!

Being imprisoned would cause many people to become bitter or to give up, but Paul saw it as one more opportunity to spread the Good News of Christ. Paul realized his current circumstances weren't as important as what he did with them. This is the same Paul who was

Saul, persecuted the church in Jerusalem, and personally witnesses the martyrdom of Stephen.

Turning a bad situation into a good one, Paul reached out to the Roman soldiers who made up the palace guard and encouraged those Christians who were afraid of persecution. We may not be in prison, but we still have plenty of opportunities to be discouraged—times of indecision, financial burdens, family conflict, church conflict, the loss of our jobs, or as in my case, the estrangement from my entire family and loss of all my possessions. How we act in such situations will reflect what we believe.

The human mind is such an interesting and fascinating thing. Like I have stated a lot so far we are all unique individuals. We are all different. God has made us all different for a reason. He has given each and every one of us different interests. Some may be attracted to history, science fiction, drama, the arts, the renaissance or whatever it may be, it is for a reason.

We have interests we can absorb ourselves into. We learn and gain knowledge. This is why controlling and abusive churches are detrimental to the growth of an individual. It makes the individual conform to a mold where God can not develop a person's individuality. OOOHHH, now that is a powerful statement.

We are also spiritual beings, God gave us a soul. In Genesis it says "and God breathed into them life." Within our soul is our Core Value, it is what we are. Our Core Value molds us and it molds our character. It gives us our convictions. Out of this we draw integrity, honesty, and convictions. We learn and it is stored in our minds.

God's gift to us is our soul; we often refer to it as our heart. We hear the comments "they have a good heart, they have a caring heart." I believe where we error, is when we let the information we gain and all of this knowledge stay in our minds and we never let it penetrate our hearts. We hear the term "head knowledge" literally we have learned this stuff and it is in our mind, in our brain so to say. We need to let the heart in on it.

When we are abused or violated it affects our heart. The pathway leading from our mind to our heart is interrupted. The bridge is destroyed. It's like a bomb goes off and just destroys the bridge from our mind to our heart. Our feelings may be hurt and or wounded.

I believe in each and every one of us, lays the answers to our hurt, our heart, or our Core Value. We all can learn from what God gave us as knowledge. The key is letting it get to our hearts. We can heal from what information we have gathered in our knowledge; if we can only get it into our hearts.

This is the key. Most often we close ourselves out from the very things we possess, which will enable us to be healed!

In my life, history is what interests me the most. I have learned a great deal from history. It was this very interest which led me to do the traveling I did in other parts of the world. Like I stated I was fascinated and interested in Eastern Europe. History of the wars and other things pertaining to this region of the world are what spurred me to learn.

It is what I learned from reading and traveling why I am able to see now and apply to my life, which has enabled me to begin and continue to heal. In writing all of this material, it has brought forth a tremendous amount of healing. My writing has been very therapeutic for me. It is as if God himself is "sweeping "my soul clean.

I feel clean inside. So much has been released within my heart and soul, which has brought me healing. My ultimate prayer and desire is through my personal healing you may find what it is, which can lead you to your healing in your lives. If my words can reach one individual then I have accomplished something great and I will consider my life to be a success.

"Go home and love your family/"

Chapter Eleven:
Rebuilding life's "soul bridge" is through Love

"Even in the most absurd, painful and dehumanized situation, life has potential meaning and therefore, even suffering is meaningful."
-Victor Frankl.

The "soul bridge" I refer to is the one I spoke of in the previous chapter, which links our brain to our heart. Dr. Viktor Emil Frankl, M.D., Ph.D. was born on March 26, 1905, in Leopoldstadt, Vienna [1].

He died on September 2, 1997 in Vienna. Frankl was an Austrian neurologist and psychiatrist as well as a World War II Holocaust survivor. Frankl was the founder of Logotherapy, which is a form of Existential Analysis.

His best-selling book, Man's Search for Meaning, which was published under a different title in 1959: *From Death-Camp to Existentialism* chronicles his experiences as a concentration camp inmate. His book describes his psychotherapeutic method of finding meaning in all forms of existence, even the most sordid ones; thus a reason to continue living.

Frankl was one of the key figures in existential therapy and a prominent source of inspiration for humanistic psychologists. On September 25, 1942 he, along with his wife, and his parents were deported to the Theresienstadt concentration camp.

There Frankl worked as a general practitioner in a clinic until his skill in psychiatry was noticed, when he was asked to establish a

special unit to help newcomers to the camp overcome with shock and
grief.

He later set up a suicide watch unit [4], and all intimations of
suicide were reported to him. To maintain his own feeling of being
worthy of his sufferings in the dismal conditions, he would frequently
march outside and deliver a lecture to an imaginary audience about
"Psychotherapeutic Experiences in a Concentration Camp".

He believed by fully experiencing the suffering objectively, he
would thereby end it.[5] Though assigned to ordinary labor details until
the last few weeks of the war; Frankl was assisted by Dr. Leo Baeck
and Regina Jonas among others. They tried to cure fellow prisoners
from despondency and prevent suicide.

He worked in the psychiatric care ward, headed the neurological
clinic in block B IV, and established and maintained a camp service of
psychic hygiene and mental care for the sick and those who were weary
of life.

While at Theresienstadt, Frankl also gave lectures on topics like
Sleep and its Disturbances, Body and Soul, Medical Care of Soul,
Psychology of Mountaineering, Rax and Schneeberg, How I keep my
nerves healthy, Existential Problems in Psychotherapy, and Social
Psychotherapy.

On July 29, 1943, he organized a closed event of the Scientific
Society. Then on October 19, 1944, he was transported to Auschwitz
concentration camp. He was processed there and spent a number of
days, [6] and then was moved to Türkheim, another Nazi concentration
camp affiliated with Dachau. He arrived at Dachau on October 25,
1944, and was to spend 6 months and 2 days working as a slave-laborer.

Meanwhile, his wife had been transferred to the Bergen-Belsen
concentration camp. The Nazi's murdered her there; his father passed

away of pulmonary edema and pneumonia in Theresienstadt camp. His mother was sent to Auschwitz from Theresienstadt and was murdered there as well.

On April 27, 1945, Frankl was liberated by the Americans. Among his immediate relatives, the only survivor was his sister, who had escaped by immigrating to Australia.

It was due to his and others' suffering in these camps he came to his hallmark conclusion

"Even in the most absurd, painful and dehumanized situation, life has potential meaning and therefore, even suffering is meaningful."

This conclusion served as a strong basis for Frankl's Logotherapy. An example of Frankl's idea of finding meaning in the midst of extreme suffering is found in his account of an experience he had while working in the harsh conditions of the Auschwitz concentration camp.

In reading Viktor Frankl's memoirs, this time has been instrumental in God speaking to me in my darkest and most hurtful moments. After reading this, my whole outlook on life and how I want to spend my remaining years has been totally reshaped and transformed.

In his memoirs Frankl states:

"We stumbled on in the darkness, over big stones and through large puddles, along the one road leading from the camp. The accompanying guards kept shouting at us and driving us with the butts of their rifles. Anyone with very sore feet supported himself on his neighbor's arm. Hardly a word was spoken; the icy wind did not encourage talk. Hiding his mouth behind his upturned collar, the man marching next to me whispered suddenly: "If our wives could see us now! I do hope they are better off in their camps and don't know what is happening to us."

Frankl went on to say,

"This brought thoughts of my own wife to mind. And as we stumbled on for miles, slipping on icy spots, supporting each other time and again, dragging one another up and onward, nothing was said, but we both knew: each of us was thinking of his wife. Occasionally, I looked at the sky, where the stars were fading and the pink light of the morning was beginning to spread behind a dark bank of clouds, but my mind clung to my wife's image, imagining it with an uncanny acuteness. I heard her answering me; saw her smile, her frank and encouraging look. Real or not, her look was then more luminous than the sun, which was beginning to rise.

At this moment a thought transfixed me: for the first time in my life I saw the truth as it is set into song by so many poets; proclaimed as the final wisdom by so many thinkers.

<u>The truth – 'love is the ultimate and the highest goal to which man can aspire.'</u>

Then I grasped the meaning of the greatest secret, which human poetry and human thought and belief have to impart:

<u>"The salvation of man is through love and in love."</u>

I understood how a man who has nothing left in this world still may know bliss, be it only for a brief moment, in the contemplation of his beloved.

In a position of utter desolation, when man cannot express himself in positive action, when his only achievement may consist in enduring his sufferings in the right way—an honorable way—in such a position man can, through loving contemplation of the image he carries of his beloved, achieve fulfillment. For the first time in my life I was able to understand the meaning of the words, "The angels are lost in perpetual contemplation of an infinite glory." [7]

Another important conclusion for Frankl was:

"If a prisoner felt that he could no longer endure the realities of camp life, he found a way out in his mental life– an invaluable opportunity to dwell in the spiritual domain, the one that the SS were unable to destroy. Spiritual life strengthened the prisoner, helped him adapt, and thereby improved his chances of survival."[8]

Frankl's concentration camp experiences thus shaped both his therapeutic approach and philosophical outlook, as reflected in his seminal publications. He often said,

<u>"Even within the narrow boundaries of the concentration camps I found only two races of men to exist: decent and unprincipled ones."</u>

These were to be found in all classes, ethnicities, and groups.[9] Following this line of thinking, he once recommended the Statue of Liberty on the East Coast of the United States be complemented by a Statue of Responsibility on the West Coast, and there are reportedly plans to construct such a statue.[10]

Frankl's approach is often considered to be amongst the broad category, which comprises existentialists.[11] Frankl, "who devoted his career to a study of an existential approach to therapy, has apparently concluded "the lack of meaning is the paramount existential stress." To him, existential neurosis is synonymous with a crisis of meaninglessness".[12]

He is thought to have coined the term 'Sunday Neurosis" referring to a form of depression resulting from awareness in some people of the emptiness of their lives once the working week is over.[13] [14] this arises from an existential vacuum, which Frankl distinguished from existential neurosis.[15]

The existential vacuum - or, as he sometimes terms it, "existential frustration" - is a common phenomenon and is characterized by the subjective state of boredom, apathy, and emptiness. One feels cynical, lacks direction and questions the point of most of life's activities. Some complain of a void and a vague discontent when the busy week is over (the "Sunday neurosis"). [15]

How do you go on when the devastation hits your life? Everyone will suffer somewhat in this life, to varying degrees and to varying extents. In order to go on, you have to rebuild the "soul bridge," which the enemy has just blown up with a nuclear bomb. Each of us will suffer hurt. As a parent, my goal was to always try and minimize the magnitude and the severity of the bomb, which would be detonated in my children's life. I never expected or realized my wife would be one of the ones who would light the fuse of my children's life bomb, which would explode on them.

I sit and think of everything I have had to deal with over these past four years. Then I research and see what Viktor Frankl and others dealt with and my trauma seems so minute in comparison. When I was reading and researching material for this part of the book, the words of Victor Frankl crushed my heart. There was nothing I could add to this chapter than already has been recorded. I want to repeat the words journaled in Victor Fankl's memoirs and end this chapter with his powerful statement concerning love.

"At this moment a thought transfixed me: for the first time in my life I saw the truth as it is set into song by so many poets; proclaimed as the final wisdom by so many thinkers.

The truth – 'love is the ultimate and the highest goal to which man can aspire.'

Then I grasped the meaning of the greatest secret, which human poetry and human thought and belief have to impart:

<u>The salvation of man is through love and in love.</u>

I understood how a man who has nothing left in this world still may know bliss, be it only for a brief moment, in the contemplation of his beloved."

After reading this chapter, if anyone has suffered more or has any complaints about any injustice they have received, please email me at helpforvictims@yahoo.com.

Notes Chapter 11:

[1] Prof. Dr. Klaus Lohrmann *"Jüdisches Wien. Kultur-Karte"* (2003), Mosse-Berlin Mitte gGmbH (Verlag Jüdische Presse)

[2] Seidner, Stanley S. (June 10, 2009) "A Trojan Horse: Logotherapeutic Transcendence and its Secular Implications for Theology". *Mater Dei Institute*. p. 2.

[3] Pytell, Timothy (1997). "Was nicht in seinen Büchern steht or Vienna's 'ideal' ehrenbürgerschaft". *Werkblatt: Zeitschrift für Psychoanalyse und Gesellschaftskritik* 39.

[4] *"The Nazis sought to prevent Jewish suicides. Wherever Jews tried to kill themselves - in their homes, in hospitals, on the deportation trains, in the concentration camps - the Nazi authorities would invariably intervene in order to save the Jews' lives, wait for them to recover, and then send them to their prescribed deaths."* – Konrad Kwiet, "The Ultimate Refuge: Suicide in the Jewish Community under the Nazis" in *Leo Baeck Yearbook, vol. 38* - 1993, p. 138.

[5] Seidner, Stanley S. (June 10, 2009) "A Trojan horse: Logotherapeutic Transcendence and its Secular Implications for Theology". *Mater Dei Institute*. P. 23.

[6] Pytell, Timothy (April 2000). "The Missing Pieces of the Puzzle: A Reflection on the Odd Career of Viktor Frankl" (fee required). *Journal of Contemporary History* 35 (2): 281–306.doi:10.1177/002200940003500208.

[7] Man's *Search for Meaning*, Part One, "Experiences   in a Concentration Camp", Viktor Frankl, pages 56-57 in the Pocket Books edition; ISBN 978-0- 671-02337-9

[8] *Man's Search for Meaning*, Part One, "Experiences in   a Concentration Camp", Viktor Frankl, p. 123

[9] *Man's Search for Meaning*, Part One, "Experiences in   a Concentration Camp", Viktor Frankl, p. 137

[10] Statue of Responsibility Foundation

[11] Yalom, Irvin D. (1980). *Existential Psychotherapy*. New York: BasicBooks (Subsidiary of Perseus   Books, L.L.C.. p. 17. ISBN 0-465-02147-6. Note: The copyright year has not changed, but the book remains in print.

[12] Yalom, Irvin D. (1980) p.421 (italics in original)

[13] Boeree, C. George (2006). "Viktor Frankl". Shippensburg University. Retrieved 7 March 2008.

[14] Seidner, Stanley S. (June 10, 2009) "A Trojan Horse: Logotherapeutic Transcendence and its Secular Implications for Theology". *Mater Dei Institute*. p 32.

[15] Yalom, Irvin D. (1980) p.449

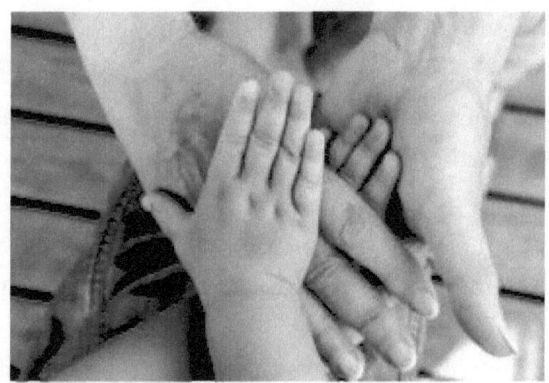

Chapter Twelve:
"Love your enemies!

"Do well and good to them. Lend to them without expecting to be repaid. Then your reward from heaven will be very great, and you will truly be acting as children of the Most High, for He is kind to those who are unthankful and wicked. You must be compassionate, just as your Father is compassionate." – Jesus Christ, Luke 6:35-36

The day arrived, which I had anticipated with so many mixed emotions, court ordered depositions. Here I was about to sit across a conference table from the man and woman who had caused all my grief with their unorthodox counseling.

I entered the room and there he sat. For weeks I had been praying and asking anyone and everybody I came into contact with to keep me in their prayers. Prayers I would conduct myself properly and in a gracious manner.

As the day progressed and carried into the second day, I discovered I was not encountering hatred, resentment, and any other host of negative, ugly feelings and emotions. Day one I witnessed the deposition of the wife. Day two I witnessed the deposition of the man.

What I began to sense and what began to overtake my mind, and the deepest depths of my heart was overwhelming pity and remorse. I found myself sitting there saying to myself,

"This guy has no clue how he is hurting people, tearing up families, and dividing homes. If he does, then he is masking it well."

I felt the inexpressible love of God for these people. I knew then and there, I was firmly on this journey, and God wanted this man to stop. The heart of God ached, and like I told another family affected soon after

"God is answering your prayers right now. He has heard all your prayers and the heartache you have been experiencing along with others, right at this moment."

I sat there looking across the table while taking notes; I thought about the three days I spent in jail. This occurred at the same time my attorney was firing questions at Knox about the same subject. Then it was if I could see my Lord, nailed on the cross, looking down on those who were crucifying Him and then looking up uttering the words of,

"Father forgive them, for they know not what they do,"

Jesus was praying to his Father, God himself, as He (Jesus) hung there and gave his life.

Then I heard Dan, my attorneys say to Knox,

"Did you have compassion on Steve Skotko as he sat in jail?"

"You say you have compassion for people, those you counsel, did you have compassion for Steve Skotko as he sat in jail?'

"Did you'" raising his voice, "Did you?" "Answer my question, did you Mr. Knox?"

These questions were flying around the conference room, as I was thinking about my incarceration concerning this case and while taking notes. I remember being in the jail cell and coming out the second day to get my meal or take my shower and It feeling like walking out of a cloud of love and the presence of God. I remember wanting to just get back into that cell, and back into to the arms of God.

When my attorney began raising his voice, I remember coming around and seeing him and Mr. Knox lifted off of their chairs and pointing at each other. Both intense, and both ready to have it out. The opposing attorney quickly took a break and left the room with Mr. and Mrs. Knox.

As the days passed from the encounter of the depositions, I was constantly reminded of the story of Corrie ten Boom. Corrie ten Boom is second only to Anne Frank as a famous female who endured and survived the Nazi Holocaust of the Jewish people in World War II.

Corrie authored the book "The hiding place." The book was later made into a full length feature film in 1975. The Dutch city of Haarlem is home to a museum where the life and efforts of Corrie ten Boom and her Family for Jewish resistance and hiding of the Jewish people for Nazi Germany resides.

After World War II, Corrie ten Boom taught the Christian gospel all over the world In telling her story, and the miracle she received and witnessed during the War. Corrie's emphasis was always on forgiveness.

In 1974 Corrie wrote the book entitled *Tramp for the Lord*. This book speaks about her teaching the Gospel of Jesus Christ in over 60 countries following the war. It was one event she spoke of, which was brought to my attention as I was sitting in my attorney's conference room.

Corrie ten Boom spent years in the Ravensbruck camp. Corrie ten Boom and her entire family were arrested by the German Gestapo in December of 1944 for aiding and hiding Jews. Corrie's father died 10 days following the family's incarceration at Scheveningen prison.

Corrie's sister Nollie, brother Wilhelm and Nephew Peter were all released. Corrie and her sister Betsie were eventually sent to the Vught political concentration camp in the Netherlands. They were then sent to Ravensbruck women's camp in Germany on December 16, 1944. Corrie's sister Betsie died in Ravensbruck.

Corrie would come to find out later her release from this camp was a clerical error, and a week after her release all other women inmates in the camp were put to death by gas chamber. Ravensbruck was not a traditional concentration camp, but it did have a gas chamber.

While teaching in Germany in 1947 she was approached by a man. When she looked up she saw standing there the man, the cruelest of all the prison guards of Ravensbruck, who had inflicted countless pain and torture on her. In her book *Tramp for the Lord*. Corrie states,

"I was reluctant to forgive him as he extended his hand to me. For a long moment we grasped each other's hands, the former prison guard, and the former prisoner. It was in that moment I have never felt the Love of God as intensely as I did then. I forgave him for all he had done, and God's peace came over me."

In the same passage of her book, in which Corrie wrote about forgiving the SS guard. Corrie wrote, in all of her post-war experiences with other victims of Nazi brutality, it was those who were able to forgive who were best able to rebuild their lives.

In closing this research, Israel has named Corrie ten Boom as a person who is Righteous Among the Nations. She was also Knighted by the Queen of the Netherlands in recognition of her work with the Dutch Resistance during World War II.

I hope I am able to convey to any victims reading these words how crucial and important it is for you to forgive. Forgiving your perpetrators is important in your recovering from being a victim.

I believe we can conquer every hurt and betrayal we experience in life. The power of the shed blood of Jesus Christ can overcome any obstacle in life. No matter what you may be forced to endure, Jesus can set you free. Forgiveness is a huge step in healing. The first thing Jesus did after he was publicly whipped, betrayed, and nailed to the cross was to forgive, first the thief, then humanity.

Those who abuse drugs, alcohol, gambling, or sexual addictions are taught they will always be this way when they seek help through the traditional 12 step recovery and abuse programs. I believe we can change. I believe we can be totally set free and the injustices we endure will make us into a better, stronger individual. I believe we can be free, and the effects will no longer seek to control our heart, mind, and soul.

If our focus is placed upon the opportunity to get stronger as a result of our failure and weakness instead of how weak we are because of our failure or weakness, then there is no mountain we cannot conquer in life.

There is life in a personal relationship with Jesus our Savior. We may not always understand things, or why things transpire the way they do, but God is in complete control of everything, and He keeps real good books.

I empathize with those who are suffering and trying to become free from all forms of abuse. I sympathize with those who are victims of abuse. It is my whole reason and motivation for writing this book. It is my hope my recovering from psychological, spiritual, and emotional abuse can be of help to any and all who are reading this. I believe 12 step programs are good and they have helped a lot of people recover from addiction. I also believe we can be totally free. We become a new creature, a new creation!

I never ever thought what happened to me ever would. I never expected the people I loved the most in this world would do the things they did and continue to do them. I will never stop loving any of them; on the contrary, I love them more. As painful and hurtful as this experience has been for me, I firmly believe today more than any other, I was chosen for such a day as this to walk in Gods divine plan. I know beyond a shadow of doubt it will lead many to a place where the Lord can heal them.

I believe in the power of God. I do not doubt any ones addictions are false, misrepresented, or misconstrued. When we learn to face our fears, then and only then will we be free from the oppression those fears bring into our lives. I believe in miracles! If we trust and believe God is in control in the joyous and good times, then we must also believe He is in control in the painful and hurtful times as well. No questions; no doubts, this is what faith is.

Nothing just happens!

God has His grand design on all of it. My job is very simple, it is

Only to believe!

In September of 2008 God began to take me on the greatest journey of my life. It has been a journey of which I would not want my darkest enemy to endure. I have literally received miracles every day since. My journey has taken me to my deepest depths of faith. I have known fear, anguish of soul, pain, shock, unbelief, betrayal on numerous occasions, and doubt, like I never knew existed. God has enriched my life to come into contact with so many awesome, loving, supportive people. I would never have met these people had I not gone through what I have.

I have also come to experience faith, hope, love, giving, compassion empathy, sympathy, and forgiveness, like I never have before. I love the Lord Jesus my Savior with my whole heart. I am so thankful, honored, and appreciative He chose me for this journey, chosen to partner with me on this road, and mission in life. What an awesome experience to be a part of so many people's lives who have been healed through this and those still to be healed.

I have been stretched to my limits. There have been times where I would lie in bed and pray I could die. I have cried so emotionally at times I could not breathe through my nose. I have felt so drained of life and exhausted at times I would think, "What's the use;" yet I would awake and feel totally refreshed the next day.

I have experienced a total peace "which goes beyond all understanding" in my life. Others who have rallied behind me and have stepped into my life to be a tremendous strength and backbone to me have said the same to me. This I received as confirmation; I am on the right track. God has led me to be friends with new people. People so awesome, when I met them I would feel I had known them my whole life.

I have met the opposition head-on, face-to-face and watched as God worked miracles in my life. I have had finances super naturally come into my life to help. I even have had a divine intervention where I firmly believe God sold a vehicle for me; literally bringing people knocking on my door without any advertising whatsoever.

Every day the pages of my life turn and I do not know where it will end. One thing which has been a constant is the Love of God and His divine provision He has given me. The Lord has sustained me and His provision is over my life. As my journey continues, people rally to my support. Past friends have been reintroduced into my life in Pueblo, Colorado. These have come to my aide; they phone and text me encouraging words and prayers of support.

I have literally stared my enemy in the face and watched as those oppositions have backed down. Those have been enemies in my flesh and enemies in the spirit. God's power is greater than any force, circumstance, and encounter any of us may face in life. They are lions with a roar, but no teeth!

My prayer and desire is my experiences, circumstances, adventures on my journey, and the outcomes of my ordeal will encourage you to believe God for greater things in your life no matter what the circumstance you face.

I want you to walk away with hope and encouragement to face your journey with a fresh view and renewed spirit. If you can grasp the concept that nothing just happens and there is a purpose for everything, then you will know that you will come out of every ordeal a better person, and others will be set free because you have!

<u>Go forward and become someone's miracle!</u>

<u>Chapter Thirteen:</u>
A Closing Word of Encouragement

"Your greatest life messages and your most effective ministry will come out of your deepest hurts."- Rick Warren

Pain is the plow used to turn up the fallow ground of our lives. These can be areas long forgotten over time. In some instances this pain can be a tragedy; maybe the loss of a loved one, or some other event, which leaves you with a feeling of being robbed of something precious.

Some individuals suffer from a huge betrayal by a spouse, friend, or other family member. No matter where we are in the pain of our situation, physical, mental, or psychological, God will always show us someone who has endured or is enduring more than we are!

I emphatically believe this! I believe God permits pain and painful experience to draw us closer to him. Something beautiful begins to happen in our lives through pain and subsequent grieving over the situation. I believe legalism and legalistic atmospheres can cause us to not fully progress though the grieving process.

Usually the thing we feel would help us the most turns out to be the vehicle which hinders us the most.

Like I stated earlier, most of the time grieving can be misdiagnosed as depression. Depression is part of grieving. With grieving comes depression. Knowing this will help you to realize, this depression will soon abate as the grieving process plays out. How long a person grieves is up to the individual. For some, they choose for it to never end, for others it can be a short time.

The Bible, especially the Old Testament, is full of stories of tragedies, and then the subsequent grieving of the people over time. In many cases the children of Israel would fast after a tragic event or the death of a heroic leader. In the process of healing, grieving is the fertilizer, which is spread over the freshly plowed land through pain. This fertilizer causes the freshly plowed land of our hearts to become fertile again.

When God shows us others who are suffering in a greater capacity than us, He is showing us He is the author of the situation. God permitted it to happen. Remember nothing just happens. Our pain and painful situations are ordained by God. This is faith.

When we come to God for salvation through the blood of Jesus, He sets us on a grand and masterful journey. It is a lifetime of events where He is working His perfect will for our lives. It is a journey unlike anyone else's where God himself is molding and shaping our lives for eternity.

Larry Johnson is quoted as stating,

"No matter what problems you're going through don't forget, a pretty rose has thorns around it and honey is guarded by bees. Both show that there is pain before gain. This is your year for reversal. Bad situations will be reversed and losses soon returned. Don't live in fear. God is giving you this year."

Yes, God is giving you this year and every subsequent year. He is creating in you something so precious, words cannot explain it.

The late David Wilkerson wrote the following,

"Paul wrote in 2 Corinthians the following,

We should not trust in ourselves. We need to trust in God who raises the dead. In essence, 'The Lord brought me to the end of all human help, to the brink of death. It was a place so hopeless, only the God of resurrection power could have rescued me!"

Remember this, Paul was Saul of Tarsus who killed and persecuted the early followers of Jesus.

Wilkerson goes on to say,

"What a wonderful place to be, at the end of your rope! I have always said when you hit rock bottom, you bump into God! Yet, if you listen to most Christians in the midst of his or her suffering, you hear, 'I'll make it somehow. I'm hanging in there. I just live one day at a time.' Since childhood most Christians have been spoon-fed the concept of self-sufficiency: 'take it like a man, and men don't cry. They never learn to trust God."

How many times have you tried to work out your own troubles?

How often have you been flooded with temptations that overwhelmed you?

Please don't misunderstand me. I believe God wants us to fight the good fight of faith. But the Lord has a way of allowing us to be 'pressed out of measure.' Nothing you try works! Nothing, you have read seems to help. No counsel of others makes sense. Suddenly, you are forced into a crisis, which obliterates all of your trust in yourself. You have no hope, except to give up all human hope. You are forced to trust God and you see the only way out of your situation is to trust.

This is a vulnerable place to be. It is in these times when God is pulling out of you, your best. Does it hurt, is it painful? You bet it is. It is in these times when 'professionals' tend to prescribe medications in an attempt to alleviate the pain. This has devastating effects on our healing!

Wilkerson also says, "Paul is clearly saying to us,

"I had the sentence of death in me."

I was tested beyond measure, at the end of all hope. It was all so I would no longer trust in myself. I had to turn to God with faith, believing He alone could save me out of my sufferings!"

I Corinthians 10:13

"The temptations in your life are no different from what others experience. God is faithful. He will not allow the temptation to be more

than you can endure. When you are tempted, He will show you a way
out so that you can endure."

What is this way of escape?

It is coming to the end of your own strength and turning
absolutely to God! It is saying, as Paul did,

"I do not trust in myself anymore!"

No more pulling up the anchor and allowing yourself to drift. The way
of escape is simple; it is a childlike faith in God. Escape is in trusting
God totally to see you through it all, resigning yourself and saying,

'God, I put everything on you!'

As you finish this book, I want to encourage you to set your life
on a better track than it was when you began reading. Trust God with
your whole heart. Trust in all the events of your life, the good, bad,
emotional, loss, victories, defeats, betrayals, and every other experience
as God making you a better person. He is making you a more complete
person, an empowered person. He has a magnificent plan for your life!

Nothing just happens, it is all for a reason!

When we allow Jesus to be Lord of all, when we cast all our
cares upon Him, fully trusting in His Word and resting in His Love; our
appearance should undergo a deep change. A quiet calm should begin to
radiate from our confidence. A peace will ooze out of us; in our
countenance, in our voice, and in our expressions.

Wilkerson further states,

"I am convinced we have a duty to let our countenance speak of God's faithfulness in our lives. People will begin to draw strength from us. But the problem is for the most part it does not. Our facial features and our body expressions will say the exact opposite.

Many believers' faces say,

"My God has failed me."

"He does not care for me anymore."

"Why did He let this happen to me?"

"I have to carry my burdens and problems alone because God doesn't come through for me anymore?"

You may not consciously say these things to yourself but they will show on your face, in your actions, and in the words you speak.

<u>Psalm 77: 2-10 says,</u>

"*[2] When I was in deep trouble, I searched for the Lord.
All night long I prayed, with hands lifted toward heaven,
but my soul was not comforted.*
[3] I think of God, and I moan, overwhelmed with longing for his help.

[4] You don't let me sleep. I am too distressed even to pray!
[5] I think of the good old days, long since ended,
[6] when my nights were filled with joyful songs.

I search my soul and ponder the difference now.
[7] Has the Lord rejected me forever?
Will he never again be kind to me?
[8] Is his unfailing love gone forever?
Have his promises permanently failed?"
[9] Has God forgotten to be gracious?
Has he slammed the door on his compassion?

[10] And I said, "This is my fate;
the Most High has turned his hand against me."

Yet the psalmist eventually comes out of his trouble with his happy countenance restored. Why? It is because he says, 'I cried out to God with my voice. In the day of my trouble I sought the Lord!'

If this describes you, I ask you; today this very day, get alone somewhere with the Lord and cry out to him. Tell Him you are at the end of your rope. Tell him you cannot take it anymore. Tell him you are ready to lay it all on His shoulders. Thank God I had a friend who told me this early on!"

If you do not know Jesus as your Lord and Savior, ask him today to forgive you. He will help you. Pray this prayer:

"Jesus, I ask you to come into my heart. I ask you to be my Lord and Savior. I believe you died for my sins. I believe you came to live among us. I believe you freely gave your life for me. I believe your shed blood sets me free from my sin. I believe you died on the cross for me. In Jesus name I pray. Amen

I want to help you. I want to help you if you just prayed this prayer and asked Jesus into your heart. I can't help you if I don't know who you are. Please send me an email @ helpforvictims@yahoo.com.

Leave me your contact information. I want to help you find a good church or ministry where you can get some support.

Please visit us at www.aheartheldransomed.com

In closing I want to say:

The Psalmist says in Psalms 199:105 the following:

*Your word is a lamp to guide my feet
and a light for my path. (NLT)*

I don't think we would need a lamp if every experience was going to be lit, and we would clearly see the way and the answers. No, it means we will face times of darkness. So dark at times when we look down, we would not even see our feet let alone the path. These are times when we don't know if we are going to make it. So dark we could not see where we are walking yet alone know where we are going!

My friends, God will always make a way and He is always there to guide us! Please contact us, we want to help.